Dangerous Narratives:

Warfare, Strategies, Statecraft

Edited by Ajit Maan

Washington, D.C.

2021

NARRATIVE
NS
STRATEGIES

Edited by Ajit Maan, Ph.D.

Published by Narrative Strategies Ink

https://www.narrative-strategies.com/

Narrative Strategies comprises a coalition of scholars and military professionals involved in the non-kinetic aspects of counterterrorism, defeating violent extremism, irregular warfare, large-scale conflict mediation, and peacebuilding.

Acknowledgements: we kindly thank Pukhtoogle for authorizing us to print the image in chapter 5.

Includes bibliographical references.

ISBN: 978-0-578-81281-6 (print paperback)

1. Narrative. 2. National Security. 3. War Studies. 4. Strategic Studies. 5. Irregular Warfare.

Contents

Part III: Stability and Statecraft

Introduction

Narrative is operative at every layer of influence. Recent research in cognitive science has demonstrated the role narrative plays in human cognition, and that new knowledge ought to be reflected and engaged in influence at every level of national security. But it is not. Narrative strategies have not been applied in a comprehensive manner to American foreign policy, warfare, or statecraft.

Narrative directly impacts the threat environment whether in a physical conflict zone, or in terms of the effects of radicalization, or the interference of foreign governments in domestic politics. Therefore dominating the narrative space should be a priority. That is where non-state actors fight best. That is where foreign governments have proven effective in waging war against us without getting dirty hands. That is precisely where our enemies dominate, and no amount of firepower will create a win in that space.

The center of gravity in any conflict is the narrative space. It always has been. But in the past we have mis-identified parts for the whole; just as terrorism is only one aspect of psychological warfare, so too psychological warfare is only one aspect of Narrative Warfare. Narrative Identity Theory is the basis of Narrative Warfare. Psychological, Information, Influence, and Stability Operations, are all aspects of Narrative Warfare. They fall under its domain.

The most effective weapons in warfare have always been the ones that target the cognitive space because they are the most enduring. Kautilya in India in the 4th century BC refers to the psychologically based tactics and strategies of those before him, suggesting that the strategies may have been employed as early as 650 BC. Hits in the cognitive space were prescribed by Sun Tzu, practiced by Genghis Khan's armies, employed by Xerxes, the Persian General 2,500 years ago, by Hannibal more than 200 years before the birth of Christ. Native American tribes understood that their blood-curdling screams terrorized their enemies, thereby reducing their will to fight before the fight began. But hits in the cognitive space do more than produce a win before the bullets fly. It is a mistake to assume that narrative is only a non-kinetic strategy that belongs in the soft power toolbox. Narrative underlies any conflict, even the most kinetically oriented.

That is the topic Dr. Howard Gambrill Clark addresses in "Narrative and War." Clark is not referring to eroding the adversaries will to fight before the fight begins, but rather, he focuses on narrative strategies for conventional kinetic warfare. In front of a transnational historical backdrop of such strategy, he invites readers to participate in a thought experiment that he warns is not for the faint of heart: subversion in the rarest of events, conventional kinetic warfare. Armies against armies. Navies against navies.

Contemporary adversaries of the United States are not eager to engage us in the kinetic realm and they haven't had to. They have cost us blood and treasure, they have waited us out, they have caused division in our homelands, and they have used our own actions against us in a way that has won them recruits. All this despite the fact that we have kinetic superiority.

This is precisely the point Col. Brian Steed, Ph.D., makes in the chapter, "Narrative Leads Kinetic Warfare," in which he demonstrates how weaker actors with a better grasp of the narrative space of the conflict zone become what he terms "narrative entrepreneurs" as they expand the disruptions in the narrative-story resonance into displacement of social functions and governance. ISIS is his primary example, but he also draws examples of actions in the narrative space by Hezbollah and the Taliban.

Even when we have won a kinetic victory and taken back territory, as we have against ISIS in Iraq and Syria, but have not won the war, we have done something worse than not winning. We have driven our adversaries underground, across borders, and left them with only the irregular weapons that they use better than we do. Now we have to fight in a domain that they dominate.

The United States is engaged in Narrative Warfare with her adversaries and Narrative Warfare is *not* information warfare. Narrative Warfare is not a struggle over information; it is competition over the *meaning* of information. Nor is Narrative Warfare an ideological fight. Ideologies rarely motivate behavior until they are narrated. Ideas get their legs from narratives. Ideas have no inherent strategy, but narratives are always strategic, and they are at their most powerful when we don't know whose strategy they serve.

Ideas are conscious; narratives are less than conscious. They operate at the level of assumption. So, much of what happens in narrative conflict is happening at a less than conscious but not unconscious level. That is what makes weaponized narrative so dangerous and so insidious.

Weaponized narrative represents a deep threat to national security and international cooperation—a threat that our advanced kinetic capacity, and those of our partner nations, cannot address alone. Brigadier General Thomas Drohan, Ph.D., demonstrates how weaponized narrative strategy is an essential aspect of China's holistic approach to warfare. He does this by first tracing how Chinese disinformation collapses decision-making in an Observe, Orient, Decide and Act (OODA) loop. Secondly, he applies my narrative weaponization model (Structure, Re-Description, Internalization, Prescription©) to China's scattered mass disinformation, thereby demonstrating how extremist narratives develop. Then, China's strategy of combining the psychological effects of disinformation and the physical effects of kinetic warfare to create synergistic dilemmas that envelop opponents, is illustrated in four of many territorial disputes—Tibet, Taiwan, India and Pakistan, and Japan.

Employing the same structure, Drohan analyses "How Russia's Narratives Reorient Decision-making and Create Combined Effects" by demonstrating three ways Russian narratives weaponize information in a strategy of combined effects using the same format he uses in his Chinese study. First, he demonstrates how Russia's disinformation narrative arranges information by distorting and reorienting decision making in an Observe-Orient-Decide Act (OODA) loop. Second, he applies my model of narrative weaponization to Russia's divisive disinformation. Third, he traces the psychological effects of disinformation and the physical effects of kinetic warfare to create a synergistic combined effect, as revealed in three illustrative samples—Georgia, Ukraine and the United States.

The real power of narrative goes untapped if we think of it as simply messaging or communication. Narrative is central to cognition of the less than conscious variety as it operates at a very basic level and yet our efforts to use narrative strategically have treated narrative as a conscious communication tactic. To counter this assumption and demonstrate the difference between communication and narrative, Paul Cobaugh applies the Narrative Strategies formula, "Narrative = Meaning, Identity, Content, Structure ©" to Afghan case studies and draws on his experience to compare the effectiveness of influence operations that have involved narrative to influence operations that haven't.

Dr. Aleksandra Nesic's case study of weaponization of the mythical 1389 Battle of Kosovo, "Myths, Memory and Ethnic War in the Balkans: Weaponizing the Kosovo Battle Narrative," examines the complex politization of cognitive and affective reactions to a site representing the myth of the Kosovo Battle, the profound role that the Serbian Orthodox Church had in transmitting the Battle's mythical narrative, and critical trajectories that continue to shape the present climate in the region. The interaction between nationalistic ideologies and the identities of groups in conflict facilitated high level recruitment and weaponization of people during the 1990s in the Balkans that led to communal ethnic cleansing. Her chapter exposes the deep psychological structures embedded in the narrative discourse of ethnic exclusivity and persecution and the logic of interethnic violence that follows.

The same strategies used to dominate in warfare can be used as instruments of peace, social stability, and statecraft. That is the topic of the final three chapters of this study.

In "Structuring for Success in Narrative Engagement," retired Army Civil Affairs officer Colonel Christopher Holshek draws on his own experience and a close look at the Defense, Joint, and Army concepts framing multi-domain operations to explain how the Army must embrace the cognitive realm of conflict and competition with the same seriousness, conscientiousness, and systems integrity in this century's continuous, people-centric rivalries of identity and ideas as it has in the episodic, state-on-state and force-on-force conflicts of 20th century conventional combined arms warfare. To prevail in a "continuum of competition" of an uncertain, dynamic, and ambiguous strategic and operating environment, Army "Unified Land Operations" call for more holistic, integrative leveraging of broad, whole-of-nation capabilities for success in the moral as well as material spaces. Operationalizing integrated physical and informational power, however, requires institutionalizing it. To expand multi domain operations from the physical to the psychological, the Army's view of informational power must go well beyond the conventional approach to information operations of messaging target audiences as a form of firepower—beyond information warfare to narrative warfare and engagement. From top to bottom, the Army must treat the conceptualization, organization, command and control, development, management, equipping, deployment, and employment of engagement forces as seriously as it does combat forces.

In "Rewriting the Narrative: A Path Forward for Policing," Dr. Frank Straub examines how, in the current arena of distrust, law enforcement can use strategic narratives to prevent and control crime and to stabilize communities. He encourages us to view this as a watershed moment in which we are called to re-imagine the role of the police in America and create a narrative strategy that supports and explains police strategies and actions, influencing the beliefs of the communities they serve, creating opportunities for collaborative peacekeeping at the neighborhood level, especially in those neighborhoods that have been most challenged by police conduct.

We end the volume by looking forward. David Ronfeldt and John Arquilla urge strategists to turn to a new concept for adapting U.S. statecraft to the information age—*noopolitik,* which emphasizes "soft power" as a successor to realpolitik, an aging concept that has emphasized "hard power." Noopolitik derives from recognizing the emergence of a new globe-circling realm: the noosphere—a global "thinking circuit" and "realm of the mind" enabled by the digital information revolution. As the noosphere grows, it will profoundly affect statecraft; the conditions favoring traditional realpolitik strategies will erode, and the prospects for noopolitik strategies will grow. The decisive factor in today's and tomorrow's wars of ideas is bound to be "whose story wins"—the essence of noopolitik.

U.S. adversaries already have the lead in deploying dark forms of noopolitik in the form of political warfare, weaponized narratives, strategic deception, epistemic attacks. The authors identify better ways to fight back and improve future prospects for the noosphere and noopolitik. U.S. policy and strategy should, among other initiatives, institute a requirement for regular reviews of America's information posture. Courses and curricula for teaching grand strategy should be redesigned to improve understanding about social evolution, social cognition, and strategic narratives.

Ajit Maan, Ph.D.
Founder and CEO, Narrative Strategies

Part I

Narrative in Kinetic Warfare

Chapter 1

Narrative and War

Howard Gambrill Clark, Ph.D.

Narrative and Blood and Fire

In this chapter, we look beyond the obvious of narrative and war.

We will not look to an army's will to fight, a soldier's will to kill and die, and nation's will to mobilize year after year. All of which is wrapped up into core identity and narrative. Meaning and purpose. Transcendence and sacred values. Those core principles that drive, for example, the U.S. Marines to unparalleled bravery. In the realm of narrative and war, much of this is accomplished in the years and months before war. Providing citizens and soldiers with a reason why. Even as such motivation is stretched after the first shots—through words and deeds to keep a nation and military from collapsing. Even if the cruel last stands are at the feet of irregulars and civilians.[1]

We will not look to driving terror into the minds of adversaries to stave off war altogether à la Sun Tzu and Kautilya and B.H. Liddell Hart and all the other masters of the indirect and narrative.[2] The Mongol effect of playing to the inner recesses of an enemy's limbic system to force them to freeze or flee. Words, scribes, and messengers relay horror so that future targets surrender without a fight. Deeds become stories that turn adversaries

[1] For more on transcendent narratives and will to fight, see: Ben Connable, Michael J. McNerney, William Marcellino, Aaron Frank, Henry Hargrove, Marek N. Posard, S. Rebecca Zimmerman, Natasha Lander, Jasen J. Castillo, and James Sladden, *Will to Fight: Analyzing, Modeling, and Simulating the Will to Fight of Military Units* (Santa Monica, CA: RAND Corporation, 2018), xi–iv, https://www.rand.org/pubs/research_reports/RR2341.html; H. Von Dach, *Total Resistance* (Switzerland: Snowball Publishing, 1957), Closing Remarks; Scott Atran, "Episode 03: Scott Atran–Sacred values," Fuuse, uploaded on June 28, 2018, https://www.youtube.com/watch?v=hWLUbHPggKI&feature=youtu.be; Scott Atran, "Analysing the limits of rational choice in political and cultural conflict," World Economic Forum, uploaded on February 14, 2017, https://www.youtube.com/watch?v=SxDS2g4qSO8&feature=youtu.be; MG Colin Gubbins, *The Art of Guerrilla Warfare*, U.K. Special Operations Executive, likely written between 1920 and 1940, pp. 39–40.

[2] Kautilya Chanakya, *Kautilya's Arthashastra*, translated by R. Shamasastry (CreateSpace Independent Publishing Platform, 2016), 540; B. H. Liddell Hart, *Strategy* (London: Faber & Faber Ltd, 1967), 361–70; Shawn Conners, editor, *36 Stratagems*, in *Military Strategy Classics of Ancient China*, translated by Chen Song (Special Edition Books, 2013). The latter was originally *The Thirty Six Stratagems*, taken from *The Book of Qi*, formally written during the Southern Qi Dynasty (400 AD). See also Angelo Codevilla, "Political Warfare: A set of means for achieving political ends," *Strategic Influence: Public Diplomacy, Counterpropaganda, and Political Warfare*, edited by J. Michael Waller (Washington, DC: Institute of World Politics Press, 2008); Flavius Mauricius Tiberius Augustus, *Maurice's Strategikon: Handbook of Byzantine Military Strategy*, translated by George T. Dennis (Philadelphia: University of Pennsylvania Press, 1984), 83–92; Lawrence Freedman, *Strategy: A History* (New York: Oxford University Press, 2013), xi–xiii, 42–53.

feckless ahead of an invading force. Such an aspect of narrative and war occurs often in the realm of deterrence—specifically to conjure psychological effects beyond the initial value of hard power and lethal force. And deterrence occurs to stave off war.[3]

We will not look to rote military deception and operational security. Military deception and operational security do not necessarily equate to strategic psychological and narrative warfare. Instead, military deception and security are normal and expected duties of every military and intelligence mission at the tactical, operational, and strategic level. Today most military units throughout the world demand every order have a deception and security plan. Without layered deception stories, feints, and fakes, an adversary will be well prepared. Some strongly worded military treatises equate failure to deceive in military ops to suicide.

We will not discuss political warfare even as this phenomenon—sometimes dubbed, depending on the whims of the folks inside the Beltway, asymmetric warfare or hybrid warfare or grey-zone operations or just plain international politics—is the norm. Even though most competition and conflict in human history exists somewhere between theoretic zero (so-called peace) and theoretic full throttle (sometimes dubbed total war, even though no person or state is ever completely at war all the time).[4]

Instead we are looking at that rarest of species. The so-called conventional war. Armies against armies. Navies against navies. The sky blackened by arrows or bombers. The mud and the guts and the blood and the fire and the horror and the loss and the randomness and the inhumanity and the insanity. Once we are fully kinetic. Once the fog is thick. Sometimes there are start dates. Sometime there are end dates. Governments fall. Nations fall. New governments rise. New nations rise. And new borders drawn.

---

[3] For more on narratives of terror to deter adversaries, see: Angelo Codevilla and Paul Seabury, *War: End and Means* (Washington, DC: Potomac Books, 2006), 151–54; Jack Weatherford, *Gengis Khan and the Making of the Modern World* (New York: Three Rivers Press, 2004), 91–94, 113–15; S. C. Gwynne, *Empire of the Summer Sun: Qanah Parker and the Rise and Fall of the Comanches, the Most Powerful Indian Tribe in American History* (New York: Scribner, 2010); Molly K. McKew, "'They Will Die in Tallinn': Estonia Girds for War With Russia," Politico, uploaded on July 10, 2018, https://www.politico.com/magazine/story/2018/07/10/they-will-die-in-tallinn-estonia-girds-for-war-with-russia-218965; Vice News, "The Russians Are Coming: Estonia's National Militia," posted on December 2, 2015, https://www.youtube.com/watch?v=nhQS48vUye0.

[4] Max Boot, *Invisible Armies: An Epic History of Guerrilla Warfare from Ancient Times to the Present* (New York: Liveright Publishing Corporation, 2013); Ralph D. Sawyer, *Lever of Power: Military Deception in China and the West* (CreateSpace Independent Publishing, 2017); Ralph D. Sawyer, *The Seven Military Classics Of Ancient China (History and Warfare)* (New York: Basic Books, 2007); Ralph D. Sawyer and Mei-Chun Lee Sawyer, *The Tao of Deception: Unorthodox Warfare in Historic and Modern China* (New York: Basic Books, 2007).

In air-conditioned offices of capitals the world over scholars and advisors may assume that all that can be done has been done. Keep the war effort going. Keep the money flowing. Keep the troops fed and armed. Leave it to the Marines and soldiers and airmen and sailors and their commanders who know best. Politics has run its course and now transfers fate to the frontlines. Ready treaties, peace accords, alliances, and exit plans, and reconstruction.

After all, this is what is taught at the service and joint war colleges in the United States: how to conduct hybrid warfare, conventional war, and great power competition through only traditions instruments of state power—military, diplomacy, economy, and traditional communications and intelligence.

What has been discounted only to have to be relearned during the next war are the non-military specific means of winning during a great conflict. And I do not mean selling war bonds, growing war gardens, recruiting at high schools, or getting industry to churn out war machines. I am referring to what is commonly called the dark arts. Or political operations. Or intelligence operations. Or what the Chinese refer to as "ch'i" and the Greeks "metis." This is the shadowy world of the indirect. The unseen. The unheard. And I am not referring to assassinations, kinetic sabotage, and double and triple agents. I am not referring to small actions that a small clandestine outfit can conduct. I am, instead, referring to strategic frameworks and mindsets for an entire government and nation and her allies—or at least DOD-sized apparatus, not relegated to a small building across the river and down the valley from the central structures of military command.

More specifically, I am referring to narrative-led means to defeat an enemy strategically and enduringly after the first shots of battle are fired.

We are discussing something that is impolite at cocktail parties and on campaign trails. Something one will unlikely find front and center at war colleges—relegated to a lesson or two if at all. This is the art and science and craft of subversion.

Whatever the goal. Whether to defeat an adversary. Collapse her government. Salt the fields. Or to see an adversaries' war machines tuck tail and b-line it back to her borders. We want to do everything we can to see to the end of war. We are bound by our morals. Our values. Our laws. Our resources. Our will. And the laws of physics.

Beyond this we are bound only by our imagination. And we owe it to ourselves to expand our imagination to fit, as closely as possible, the parameters of our morals and our values and our resources and our will and the laws of physics. Echoing so many strategy writers and scholars who believe strategy is balancing ends with ways and means, famed Yale history professor John Lewis Gaddis claims in his book *On Grand Strategy*, "Means, though, are stubbornly finite: they're boots on the ground, ships in the sea, and the bodies required to fill them." Gaddis clearly understands that good strategies can get more out of the starting balance of means to conduct war. Clearly understands that even visionaries set on an ideal still must be brutally practical sometimes around changing affairs and terrains. However, like so many others, Gaddis only focuses on the means of war that we see in films. Tanks and gas and bullets et al. The invisible elephant in the room is almost limitless creativity of war activities that cost little-to-no money. Specifically narrative strategies to subvert.

But if subversion is not widely taught. If subversion is not widely understood. Then what can we do?

We can start educating ourselves and our leaders now. On this widely misunderstood concept of narrative warfare. The following is one—just one, this is not the be-all and end-all and is not meant to be exhaustive—blueprint in its bud. These comprise not strategies but instead philosophies and tradecraft that can be employed by all instrument of national power. At all levels from the technical to the tactical to the operational to the strategic.

These are not meant for the faint of heart. Nor for the commanders seeking promotion and ribbons and glory.

Szalámitaktika – Get Others to Kill for You

Set the enemy camp ablaze. Every political and social and industrial network has seams. Find those narrative—motivation, identity, meaning, and purpose—seams and exacerbate them. Through intermediaries, proxies, and every subtle and clandestine channel collapse the adversary from within.

Hungarian gave us the term *szalámitaktika*—literally salami tactics, even as there is nothing tactical about it—to describe inspiring enemies to fight one another and factions within enemy camps to fight each other kinetically and by all other means. Although the term often conjures ideas of *divide et impera* (divide and conquer), it may be enough sometimes to divide in order to degrade and distract.

Fifth Columns and Fellow Travelers—Warfare through Proxies by Invisible Means

Popularized by a Spanish General and Ernest Hemingway, fifth columns can refer to those in an adversarial state that will fight or enable your forces when you enter enemy terrain. Over the decades, we have used this word to more broadly refer to networks in militaries, militias, societies, and industries whose goals are in consonance with yours.

Fellow travelers, during the Cold War, generally referred to political figures and intellectuals in the enemy camp whose ideas were in consonance with that of other side. Whose influence was increased through indirect funds, grants, and sometimes simple access (inviting scholars to Moscow to conduct interviews and publish books, for example). Many of these individuals were deeply patriotic. For example, there may be a scholar or journalist in the United States who truly believes that de-nuclearization was a first step toward peace but has no love for the Soviet and his crimes against humanity. But whose ideas could still further the agenda of Moscow.[5] Today, fellow travelers in literature may refer to any influential person abroad whose ideas, narratives, and networks may align with the national interests of the United States.

To underline fifth columns and fellow travelers to effect *szalámitaktika,* I have my students imagine they are charged with commanding an army of country *x* to invade Iran and topple the government in Tehran. This would be a horrific idea for any government, especially the United States. The destabilizing aftereffects. The extinguishing of decades searching for peace and understanding. The radicalizing of citizens otherwise uninterested in the United States, would make such an invasion ill advised, ill fated, and a quagmire not to mention human suffering, pain, and death that would be totally unnecessary. But for this thought

[5] Scott Shane, *Dismantling Utopia: How Information Ended the Soviet Union* (Chicago: Ivan D. Lee, 1994), 3–42; Lt. Gen. Ion Mihai Pacepa and Prof. Ronald J. Rychlak, *Disinformation* (Washington, DC: WND Books, 2013); Gal Beckerman, "How Soviet Dissidents Ended 70 Years of Fake News," *The New York Times*, April 10, 2017, https://www.nytimes.com/2017/04/10/opinion/how-soviet-dissidents-ended-70-years-of-fake-news.html; CIA, "Comparison of Soviet and VOA Radio Propaganda," March 21, 1951.

exercise, we are in a parallel universe. The student has her orders. And the student has elected to go ahead with plans. She only has two weeks to plan. What can she do to light Iran ablaze to ensure easier access for her tanks to roll into the capital to take out the underground bunkers of governing officials and military headquarters? As her soldiers prepare. And she coordinates with the navy and air force and overcome nearly impossible logistics challenges. And she conducts the psychological operations, military deception, and operational security schemes to throw her adversary off balance, how can her staff collapse all that is inside Iran? Perhaps she can call for Kurds to overthrow local village and town governance. LBGQT—ravaged by years of imprisonment and death—communities to provide intelligence. Sunnis to be at the ready to take over radio stations. Arab militias and volunteers to sabotage supply lines. Those 1979 revolutionary true believers, now disenchanted by a Tehran that has reneged on its promises, may be in the wings to take over. Jewish civilians may work through intermediary governments to support some protests and riots. Iran-Iraq war veterans—fed up with a government that has forgotten their sacrifices—may be influenced to provide no active help to Tehran once the incursion begins. Informal farmers' unions may be persuaded to allow foreign forces limited food supply (for money) if they thought their crops might be valued in a future government. If even one of these systems effectively rebelled against Tehran, the incursion might be easier. And much of the strength of the central government may very well be degraded or even collapsed.

Let us look to historical case studies to color in our fictional thought experiment.

Cortes and Pizarro—Collapsing Empires without Bullets

In 1519 the Aztecs were not aware of Spanish interference and control of Caribbean islands. Cortes had only 550 men, so the initial Aztec greeters saw no reason to fight them and spent time pondering whether they were a threat or benign. Hernan Cortes asked to speak to their leader on peaceful diplomatic terms. At the meeting, Cortes' men killed Emperor Montezuma's guards and staff but kept the leader alive. They kept Montezuma alive—a prisoner in his own home—and used him largely as a puppet, as if the Spaniards were still there on a diplomatic peaceful mission. During this time the Spaniards conducted a wide-ranging narrative-intelligence mission sending emissaries throughout the empire to gain intelligence on the composition, disposition, and political leaning of sects of civil society.[6] After a revolt, the Spaniards fled the capital. Understanding the disparate civil-society systems, Cortes convinced some of the subjected masses to revolt against the empire. Tens of thousands revolted against the elites thinking the Spaniards were helpful allies for self-determination. More Spaniards eventually arrived while the masses were fighting themselves materializing latent fissures. In the end the Spanish conquered and subjugated the remaining natives.[7]

A decade after the conquest of Mexico, Francisco Pizarro González conducted narrative reconnaissance missions into South America. Eventually, Pizarro used Cortes' model and with 168 men was able to infiltrate the Inca headquarters as peaceful diplomats. They kidnapped the leader and allied themselves with disparate civil-society sects. The empire flailed and weakened for follow-on Spanish conquer. The Incas were unaware of the Spanish mission in Mexico.[8]

This 'divide-and-conquer' method has been used for millennia. But it demands of intelligence services understanding not only the compositions, dispositions, strengths, and vulnerabilities of adversaries but also the intentions, goals, and motivations at the sub-group level. Intelligence must break open a state or a society and conduct 'microscopic' human terrain analysis.

Mongols and the Kaiser—Lay Waste Before Arriving

Before Genghis Khan's sons and generals entered city states from Mesopotamia to Ukraine, he would send intermediaries—trusted actors by locals of the cities he was about to enter—to influence and persuade Christians to revolt against Muslim rule, Muslims against Christian rule, plebes against rulers, the forgotten against the privileged. The enemy would be weakened or collapsed by the time of Mongol arrival if given enough time.[9]

---

[6] Yuval Nohah Harari, *Sapiens: A Brief History of Humankind* (New York: HarperCollins, 2014), 326–30.
[7] Harari, *Sapiens*, 326–30.
[8] Harari, *Sapiens*, 326–30.
[9] Richard A. Gabriel, *Genghis Khan's Greatest General: Subotai the Valiant* (Norman, OK: University of Oklahoma Press, 2004), 138–41; J. J. Saunders, *The History of the Mongol Conquests* (Philadelphia: University of Pennsylvania Press, 1971), 111–12; Jack Weatherford, *Gengis Khan and the Making of the Modern World* (New York: Three Rivers Press, 2004), 91–94, 113–15.

During the First World War, the Kaiser unleashed Vladimir Lenin on Petrograd. Not only were Eastern Front Russian troops coaxed to give up their positions, but Lenin's many revolutions pitted Russians against Russians allowing Germany to focus on the Western Front. This was a case of too little too late. Only when the Kaiser found himself cornered did he push for *szalámitaktika* that could have saved his side. And to boot, his government was too weak after the war to attempt to ease Lenin's continental overthrows that led to post-war Germany's further instability. As is common, the Kaiser elected for narrative warfare far too late, only when he was desperate. But it would be too easy to throw every decision and action out as leading to failure.

Although late in the game with a starving population and decimated resources, the Kaiser was able to take one side of the war—literally—off the table. Even when anti-Leninists later discovered that Germany continued to financially support—in part—the Marxists' propaganda, Lenin was adeptly able to dismiss claims of compromise and chalk them up to simple and practical opportunism. In effect, Lenin was able—to some—to claim that he was using Germany and not the other way around, thus eschewing some criticism. Of course, the secondary and tertiary effects included an unimaginably successful Lenin whose ideas were exported and essentially blew up in Germany's face. It is anyone's guess what Germany could have done had the Kaiser remained powerful somehow.[10]

Second World War—Set Fire to the World

In the Second World War, Great Britain sought to set "Europe ablaze" through direct and indirect support to any and every anti-Nazi faction, militia, and civilian resistance. This included institutional sabotage by which those working in factories—specifically those that did not care for the Nazi cause but felt outright rebellion—would lead to death and crackdowns that would stop further anti-Nazi efforts. Simple sabotage, currently declassified and available on the web, was one iteration of the tradecraft necessary to retard industrial effort. Cleverly disguised as good business practices, this tradecraft allowed workers and managers to slow

[10] Angelo Codevilla and Paul Seabury, *War: End and Means* (Washington, DC: Potomac Books, 2006); Angelo Codevilla, "Political Warfare: A set of means for achieving political ends," *Strategic Influence: Public Diplomacy, Counterpropaganda, and Political Warfare*, edited by J. Michael Waller (Washington, DC: Institute of World Politics Press, 2008).

down operations—sometimes to an almost standstill—through too much paperwork, needless busy work, administrative mazes, and too many middle managers. Subtle and effective, such distributed manuals allowed the everyday Jane to jam up Third Reich war machines. And the real numbers and extent to which rebellions throughout Europe quelled German strategy will unlikely ever be known as subtlety and deception have even kept historians from a complete picture.[11]

Invisible and Silent—Killing them Softly

Even today historians look to the workings of spy and sabotage networks during the U.S. War of Independence and Civil War and are faced with believable deception stories, arcane codes, and little or no paperwork as is the norm for wartime. This is one of the greatest challenges facing scholars of influence in war—how can one study what is not recorded?

And more importantly, for this chapter, why keep *szalámitaktika* hidden at all? Secrecy and layered deception stories along with trusted intermediaries are necessary so as not to inspire the enemy to learn the tradecraft and do likewise to you, so as to not allow the enemy to publicize your actions so that rebels in all shades are not targeted, so as not to take away the seeming independence from those willing to split up the enemy camp, and because often you are not the most trusted supporter. The enemy of your enemy is not necessarily your friend. Take the Iran thought project. Would any of these groups be pro-United States openly? Probably not. Overt meddling may lead to disparate groups becoming united against a common enemy. But their approximate goals may still be in consonance with yours. So subtlety is king.

As a note of warning, this is a dangerous business. History is ripe with *szalámitaktika* running afoul. Backing a drug cartel in Afghanistan—a cartel who opposes the Taliban—may very well cause people to rebel and welcome back the Taliban who may be seen as a lesser of evils. It takes a keen understanding of the core foundational narratives of potential fifth

[11] William Stevenson, *A Man Called Intrepid: The Incredible True Story of the Master Spy Who Helped Win World War II* (New York: Skyhorse Publishing, 1976), chapters 4, 5, 11, 12; Paul Kix, *The Saboteur* (New York: Harper Perennial, 2017).

columns and fellow travelers (again, the terms here are used liberally in the modern sense). What is their outlook on the world? Do they intend to bring more instability than your targeted enemy? Will they become more extreme versions of your current enemy? Will they ever stop rebelling? An insight into their collective subconscious, into their will to fight and die, into their sacred values for which they are willing to sacrifice are necessary. It is not as easy as taking a poll or survey—whose results may be worse than not knowing anything, especially as people are rarely aware of their beliefs. But just because it is difficult and requires some of the world's top narrative scholars does not mean *szalámitaktika* cannot or should not be done. It is hard work. And you will get it wrong sometimes. But the *szalámitaktika* can be as effective as a thermonuclear bomb if it collapses the enemy or at least makes the adversary weaker as she finds herself amidst dozens of lethal creatures in her own swamp, unable to fight at all or fight as well as she could.

If it's so difficult, what can warfighters learn to prepare for war? They can learn narrative warfare from narrative scholars. Today, inside the beltway and in military units the world over, some commanders and staff train with false myths.

One myth is that messaging alone works. When in fact there is no silver-bullet message. Overt messages sent into the ether have no effect. At least they have had no effect in the history of mankind. People are not like physical targets and do not easily change their minds. Instead, influence through narrative warfare is conducted indirectly and exploits ideas and networks that already exist, rather than creating new trends out of the blue.[12]

Another myth is that polling and survey data offer insight into people's minds and beliefs. In fact, decades of multiple studies in anthropology, psychology, history,

---

[12] Hugo Mercier, *Not Born Yesterday—The Science of Who We Trust and What We Believe* (Princeton: Princeton University Press, 2020), 113–17, 128–45; Joseph S Roucek, "Ideology as a Means of Social Control I," *American Journal of Economics & Sociology* 3, no. 1 (October 1943): 35–45; Joseph S. Roucek, "*Ideology as a Means of Social Control III*," *American Journal of Economics & Sociology* 3, no. 3 (April 1944): 357–70; Miguel A. L. Nicolelis, "The Human Brain, the True Creator of Everything, Cannot Be Simulated by Any Turing Machine," *Think Tank: Forty Neuroscientists Explore the Biological Roots of Human Experience*, edited by David J. Linden (New Haven: Yale University Press, 2018); Steve Ayan, "The Brain's Autopilot Mechanism Steers Consciousness: Freud's notion of a dark, libidinous unconscious is obsolete. A new theory holds that the brain produces a continuous stream of unconscious predictions," *Scientific American*, December 19, 2018, https://www.scientificamerican.com/article/the-brains-autopilot-mechanism-steers-consciousness; Leonard Mlodinow, *Subliminal: How Your Unconscious Mind Rules Your Behavior* (New York: Pantheon Books, 2012), 11–51; Daniel Kahneman, *Thinking, Fast and Slow* (New York: Farrar, Straus and Giroux, 2013); Michael Lewis, *The Undoing Project: A Friendship That Changed Our Minds* (New York: W. W. Norton & Company, 2017); Anil Seth, "Your brain hallucinates your conscious reality," TED Talks, uploaded on July 18, 2017, https://www.youtube.com/watch?v=lyu7v7nWzfo; Beau Lotto, "The Neuroscience of Creativity, Perception, and Confirmation Bias," *Big Think*, uploaded on June 28, 2017, https://www.youtube.com/watch?v=vR2P5vW-nVc.

neurobiology, psychiatry, communications, and philosophy suggest emphatically that what one says does not represent one's beliefs. Or future action. What one thinks is their belief may belie their true underlying motivations and drivers and views of the world. People are terrible at judging their own beliefs—especially those values for which to fight and kill and die. There is no quick solution. There is no formula. And quantitative analysis alone will not breed good prediction with what we know today of the human brain.[13] Instead, those steeped in the scholarship and execution of narrative warfare will be able to offer frameworks and theories that are actionable, practical, and intrepid.

Too often we wait until desperation to conduct narrative warfare. This was the case of the Kaiser sending a memo to Mexico City to attempt to get Mexico and Japan involved in the First World War. Desperate, sloppy, and not too subtle. We cannot wait until the dog days of combat to relearn, once again, narrative warfare. Instead it must be learned and wrestled with in training just as we learn good marksmanship.

---

[13] Jan Blommaert and Dong Jie, *Ethnographic Fieldwork: A Beginner's Guide* (Bristol, UK: Multilinguual Matters, 2011), chapter 1; Adam Lankford, *The Myth of Martyrdom: What Really Drives Suicide Bombers, Rampage Shooters, and Other Self-Destructive Killers* (New York: St. Martin's Press, 2013), 21–40; Daniel H. Pink, *When: the Scientific Secrets of Perfect Timing* (New York: Riverhead Books, 2018), 9–48; Peter Sheridan Dodds et al., "Temporal Patterns of Happiness and Information on a Global Social Network: Hedonometrics and Twitter," *PloS ONE* 6, no. 12 (December 2011): 1–26. Max Hastings, *Retribution: The Battle for Japan, 1944–45* (New York: Alfred A. Knopf, 2008), xvii–xxv; Mlodinow, *Subliminal*, 11–29.

Chapter 2

Narrative Leads Kinetic Warfare

Lieutenant Colonel (Retired) Brian L. Steed, Ph.D.

Battles of Mosul (2014 and 2016-2017)

Iraqi security forces attacked a home outside of Mosul on 4 June 2014. As the gunfire raged around the home, the occupant, Najm al-Bilawi al-Dulaimi, who was the reason for the attack, blew himself and the home up. The next day ISIS[14] launched the campaign, then named after al-Bilawi, that captured Mosul in just six days. From there, they declared the return of the successor of the Prophet Mohamed and the governed territory for all true Muslims, or caliphate. More than two years later, the government of Iraq, supported by a coalition of nearly eighty nations, took 278 days to recapture Mosul (refer to Figure 1). In the first instance, ISIS was outnumbered almost sixty to one, yet they took the city quickly and with little destruction of the infrastructure. In the case of the coalition, ISIS was outnumbered nearly twelve to one, and it required the damage or destruction of more than sixty percent of the city. The difference between the two battles of Mosul is the difference between narrative war and kinetic war.

The battle of Mosul in 2014 that began with an intelligence tip which resulted in the self-destruction of the ISIS leader in the city was a result of successful Iraqi security force

[14] ISIS stands for the Islamic State in Iraq and al-Sham. See Brian L. Steed, *ISIS: The Essential Reference Guide* (Santa Barbara, CA: ABC-CLIO, 2019), xi-xii, 17: "Throughout this [chapter], the term ISIS is used to identify the group from its conceptual inception at or about 1999 to the present. In reality, the group has had multiple names during that time frame. … [H]owever, to avoid confusion, the general term used will consistently be ISIS." The definition continues:

> Al-Sham is an Arabic word that dates back centuries and has multiple meanings. It is often pronounced ash-Sham, because of Arabic standard pronunciations of certain letters following the definite article. It can mean the specific city of Damascus, the greater Damascus area, the modern country and boundaries of Syria, or something called Greater Syria. This last area includes the modern states of Syria, Lebanon, Israel, most of Jordan, and portions of Turkey and Egypt. Levant is derived from Latin and French words that mean rising. Literally, it is the place where the sun rises or the east. In the case of both Latin and French speakers in the medieval period, this was a reference to the Eastern Mediterranean. In Western academic circles, the Levant includes the same general region as given in the explanation of al-Sham previously. Few Arabs use this phrase and they typically only do so in an academic setting. Both al-Sham and Levant are conceptual terms. There is no fixed border for either of the geographic designations and they do not represent a historic kingdom. It is like referring to "the south" in the United States or "the West" in terms of culture. The U.S. Obama administration labeled ISIS as the Islamic State of Iraq and the Levant or ISIL whereas ISIS referred to itself as the Islamic State of Iraq and al-Sham. Some reporters and media outlets reported ISIS as the Islamic State of Iraq and Syria. When ISIS used the term, it always used al-Sham. It has never used Levant in its name. Few Arabs have ever used ISIL as a designation because it is not reflective of the Arabic acronym for the organization here referred to as ISIS. Al-Sham is a name that has ancient connections. The Prophet Mohamed used the term. He never used Levant.

intelligence work. By the evening of 4 June 2014, Iraqi police and other security forces in Mosul had every right to consider the day a success.[15] ISIS, despite suffering a setback, continued their planning. There is discrepancy about the purpose of the attack on Mosul that began the next day. Was it punitive? Was it a part of the "breaking down the walls" campaign to release prisoners from the prison in Mosul? Was it intended to establish an ISIS foothold in the eastern part of Mosul?[16] At this point, it is probably impossible to get a factual answer.[17] Regardless, ISIS attacked several police and security force positions beginning on 5 June and continuing for the next several days.[18] ISIS demonstrated a mastery of shock tactics as they directed their early efforts against the hotel that served as the command post of the Iraqi commanding officer and detonated a massive truck bomb that effectively incapacitated the Iraqi defending leadership.[19] As the attacks continued, ISIS seemed to gain greater and greater steam and the security forces began to buckle and ultimately to flee the city after less than six full days of fighting.[20]

Mosul was a city of between one and two million people with a reported security and military force of about sixty thousand men.[21] The use of the word "reported" emphasizes that Iraqi security forces developed a habit of reporting ghost soldiers, or false soldiers, for the sake of bringing in extra cash for their reporting commanders who were responsible for distributing the monthly payroll.[22] Additionally, many soldiers who had been showing up for duty did not remain, but had been fleeing the city during the previous days, weeks, and months as a result of an aggressive and brutally graphic ISIS engagement and media campaign.[23]

---

[15] Dana J.H. Pittard and Wes J. Bryant, *Hunting the Caliphate: America's War on ISIS and the Dawn of the Strike Cell* (New York: Post Hill Press, 2019), 43.

[16] Mosul is practically two cities with the Tigris River separating them with five main bridges connecting each half. The ancient city sits along the river on the west bank along with the most significant civic institutions like the university, airport, and government buildings.

[17] Ned Parker, Isabel Coles, and Raheem Salman, "Special Report: How Mosul fell—An Iraqi general disputes Baghdad's story," *Reuters*, October 14, 2014.

[18] Pittard and Bryant, *Hunting the Caliphate,* 43.

[19] Joby Warrick, *Black Flags: The Rise of ISIS* (New York: Doubleday, 2015), 259.

[20] Suadad al-Salhy and Tim Arango, "Sunni Militants Drive Iraqi Army Out of Mosul," *The New York Times*, June 10, 2014; Parker, Coles, and Salman, "Special Report"; Warrick 2015, 258–59.

[21] One author has the numbers as 3,000 ISIS fighters against 25,000 defenders in Mosul; the better part of five Iraqi divisions. Pittard and Bryant, *Hunting the Caliphate*, 43. Other authors have it at between 400 and 1,500 ISIS fighters against 10,000. Parker, Coles, and Salman, "Special Report"; Warrick, *Black Flags*, 258–59.

[22] Parker, Coles, and Salman, "Special Report."

[23] Parker, Coles, and Salman, "Special Report"; Warrick, *Black Flags*, 259.

Figure 1: Comparison of Battles of Mosul (2014 and 2016-2017)

All numbers are estimates. The data for this table comes from a wide variety of sources and includes assessments and adjustments by the author. Simply stated, no one knows the actual numbers for any of these areas. This might be because the real numbers just are not known. It is also possible that either the Iraqi government or ISIS is inclined toward misreporting the numbers. Therefore, the numbers below are intended to provide a general tone of the battle more than precise counts. In 2014, the attacker was ISIS and the defender was the Iraqi Security Forces. In 2016-2017, the roles were reversed.

2014		2016-2017
(4+ yrs prep) 6	Days	(2+ yrs prep) 278
1,000	Attacking Force	110,000
60,000	Defending Force	9,000
1:60	Ratio of Attacker to Defender	12:1
105+	Attacking Force Killed	(possibly 3-5x) 1,400
6,500	Defending Force Killed	8,000
1:65	Ratio of Attacker to Defender Killed	(~ 1:2 to 1:1.1) 1:6
<1%	Infrastructure Damaged/Destroyed	>60%
Unknown	Civilians Killed	25,000
500,000	Civilians Displaced	900,000

ISIS probably attacked Mosul with forces initially in the hundreds and finally slightly more than a thousand.[24] None of the numbers associated with the battles for Mosul, either in 2014 or 2016-2017, can be verified, which is true for almost every statistic associated with ISIS. These are estimates. Regardless of the exact figures, the ratios are staggering (see Figure 1). This is profound displacement.

The numbers in Figure 1 compare and contrast the ISIS narrative-led attack in 2014 and the Iraq Army and U.S.-led coalition attack in 2016-2017. The ratios for the attacking Iraqi Army in 2016 are similar to what U.S. Army doctrine would recommend for an attack into a

[24] Parker, Coles, and Salman, "Special Report."

major urban area against a prepared opponent. This is what makes the ISIS success, while significantly outmanned, revolutionary.

Some claim the revolutionary success was a result of social media generating fear.[25] The social media portrayals of ISIS murders, targeted killings, executions, and drone observation probably generated fears that the group was larger than what one saw. ISIS also built upon rumors and local personal networks through its hundreds of engagements, its efforts to coerce, intimidate, and threaten people.[26] People had heard what ISIS was doing, saw it on video, and received social media posts. All of this, in combination with aggressive and prolonged violence, caused one of the largest Iraqi cities to collapse and fall into ISIS control. In the process, ISIS freed the detainees in the Badush Prison, hundreds of whom joined ISIS immediately.[27] About six hundred of the prisoners were Shia and they were driven to the desert and executed.[28]

The ISIS surge in Iraq, which had been ongoing since the middle of 2013, resumed after the capture of Mosul as the group continued to displace governance in Iraq. The displacement sometimes was as simple as government officials failing to respond to pro-ISIS rallies or processions through a city or village, as in Fallujah beginning in late-2013. It may also have been avoidance of ISIS activities, the homes of known ISIS members and leaders, or the deference to ISIS preferences or policies as regularly happened in Mosul leading up to the events described above. ISIS conducted attacks in Haditha, Abu Ghraib, Hawija, Samarra and other towns and cities before Mosul.[29] By the end of 2014, ISIS had total or near-total governance of the major cities of Ninewa, Kirkuk, Salah al-Din, Diyala, and Anbar provinces.

How did ISIS accomplish all of this success in days when state run militaries failed to demonstrate similar success in months? That is the question of 21st century conflict.

---

[25] Jessica Stern and J.M. Berger, *ISIS: The State of Terror* (New York: HarperCollins, 2015); Michael Weiss and Hassan Hassan, *ISIS: Inside the Army of Terror* (New York: Regan Arts, 2015); P.W. Singer and Emerson T. Brooking, *Like War: The Weaponization of Social Media* (New York: Houghton Mifflin Harcourt Publishing Company, 2018).

[26] Brian L. Steed, Unpublished Personal Journal of Events as a Plans Officer for the Combined Joint Land Force Component Command-Iraq (CJFLCC-I) Command, Baghdad, Iraq, 2015.

[27] Pittard and Bryant, *Hunting the Caliphate* 43.

[28] Charles R. Lister, *The Syrian Jihad: Al-Qaeda, the Islamic State and the Evolution of an Insurgency* (New York: Oxford University Press, 2015), 232.

[29] Lister, *The Syrian Jihad*, 231.

Three Years and Three Philosophies

There are three years of conflict that fit very neatly in a discussion of philosophical approaches of military conduct: 1814, 1914, and 2014 (refer to Figure 2). Each of these years can serve as a sort of description of the philosophy of the period and the major wars associated: Napoleonic wars, World War I, and the Global War on Terrorism. The three philosophies of war are maneuver, firepower, and narrative. Each is expressed in a simplified form acknowledging that much complexity is ignored in this description.

Figure 2: Three Years – Three Philosophies

	1814	1914	2014
Philosophy	Maneuver	Firepower	**Narrative**
Exemplars	Napoleon	WWI, WWII	ISIS, Russia, China
Influence by ...	Concentration	Targeting	Engagement
Maneuver is ...	Position	Physics	Cognition
Age of ...	Battles	Combat	Conflict
Must Defeat ...	Armies	States	People/Beliefs

Maneuver war is exemplified in the behavior and performance of Napoleon Bonaparte. This great historical figure dominated his age and expressed a type of warfare that seemed to convey that wars could be won by winning battles. To win those battles, Napoleon concentrated his force at a decisive point or he directed the center of gravity of his force against the center of gravity of the enemy. In that era there was a decisive point or center of gravity.[30]

---

[30] Antoine Henri Jomini used the term decisive point rather than center of gravity. He elaborated this through a series of maxims that included the following three points: "1. To throw by strategic movements the mass of an army, successively, upon the decisive points of a theater of war, and also upon the communications of the enemy as much as possible without compromising one's own. 2. To maneuver to engage fractions of the hostile army with the bulk of one's forces. 3. On the battlefield, to throw the mass of the forces upon the decisive point, or upon that portion of the hostile line which it is of the first importance to overthrow." Baron de Jomini, *Summary of the Art of War* (Philadelphia, PA: J. B. Lippincott & Co, 1862), 461. A modern edition is available, translated

A commander could concentrate or mass and then direct the mass of his army against the mass of the enemy army and by doing so might win the battle, drive the enemy from the field, cause the enemy to capitulate, and win the war under terms favorable to the victorious commander. Success came in defeating the enemy's army.

Firepower war is exemplified in the conduct of World War I and World War II. Commanders sought to influence the enemy through targeting—the right violence directed at the right part of the enemy at the right time. The violence, so directed, was typically in the form of explosive force delivered by a wide variety of platforms from land, sea, and air. Both of these wars, and the wars that have followed this paradigm, include near continuous violence for long periods of time—combat rather than battle. Though there are things called battles in the two World Wars it is rare that those battles began the violence or that the violence ended with the conclusion of the battle. The violence simply continued. Death occurred before and after the battle as is indicative of a combat environment. Success came from defeating states.

Narrative war is exemplified by ISIS, though there are many other non-state and state actors that have applied this same philosophy of war. In narrative war, influence comes through engagement—typically person-to-person engagement, though this engagement may come through social media, violent interaction, or other traditional forms of influence operations. Success in influence comes through changing individual and collective cognition. The change from maneuver to firepower saw a spreading out of the peak violence from battle that was somewhat isolated in time and space to combat which is larger and more diffused across both time and space. Narrative war is even more diffuse than combat such that the violence is more accurately expressed as conflict that, at times, remains below obvious triggers for combat and may often be characterized as competition. Success comes from defeating people and beliefs. The difficulty of defeating an ideology in combination with diffused violence makes it more likely that the conflict is nearly constant—never ending—a forever war.

---

by Capt. G. H. Mendell and Lieut. W. P. Craighill (Westport, CT: Greenwood Press, 1992). Carl von Clausewitz, on the other hand pioneered the use of the term center of gravity as stated in his quote, "One must keep the dominant characteristics of both belligerents in mind. Out of those characteristics, a certain center of gravity develops, the hub of all power and movement, on which everything depends. That is the point at which all our energies should be directed." Carl von Clausewitz, *On War*, edited and translated by Michael Howard and Peter Paret (Princeton: Princeton University Press, 1976), 595.

There is no pure maneuver war, nor is there a pure firepower war, nor is there a pure narrative war (refer to Figure 3). In every case of violent conflict, there is some combination of the three. That was true thousands of years ago when the Assyrian military machine used a story of terror to influence populations to submit, capitulate, or return to the fold. The Assyrians used violence or the firepower of their day and they used maneuver, but predominantly they relied on narrative to maintain a multi-regional empire in an era before social media or the printing press.

How does this actually work?

Figure 3: Types of War

How Narrative is the Environment of Conflict[31]

Hans Delbruck expressed in 1890 winning strategies of war as either annihilation or exhaustion. He used two German words to express these ideas that literally translate to thrashing strategy or fatigue strategy. His word *ermattungsstrategie* (literally fatigue strategy

[31] Many of these ideas are expressed in a chapter written by the author and titled "Narrative in Culture, Center of Gravity, and the Golden Azimuth," Army University Press, forthcoming.

and hereafter referred to as exhaustion) is often translated as attrition, but the argument here is that this translation is wrong as it fails to grasp the full concept of fatigue.[32] Attrition is about the destruction of enemy capability and exhaustion is about the destruction of enemy will. Delbruck used the ancient Athenian general Pericles as an example of exhaustion as he sought to defeat the Spartans in the Peloponnesian War through a form of war without battle.[33] Exhaustion, despite the sound of the word and the image it conjures of a person at the end of a marathon or some very long race, can happen quickly as well as slowly. Observe how quickly an outmatched opponent concedes a competition as a simple example. Once a person accepts that they cannot win then they move to exhaustion.

The end of World War II accomplished a couple of key things. One, it made war illegal through the acceptance of the United Nations charter.[34] Though interstate war did not end with the adoption of that charter, it is factual that interstate wars have declined and wars between Great Powers have essentially died out as have wars between Western democracies. What this means is that current conflict occurs between actors with significant obvious power discrepancies. Second, World War II introduced existential weapon capabilities that effectively created a ceiling for violence in armed conflict. Under the threat of nuclear destruction, all post-World War II conflict did and must take into account the limits created by violence potential and by international legal constraint. Firepower was ascending from World War I through the end of World War II to the point that firepower as manifested in nuclear weapons posed a global existential threat. That threat and the unique global

---

[32] Gordon A. Craig, "Delbruck: The Military Historian" in *Makers of Modern Strategy: Military Thought from Machiavelli to Hitler* (Princeton: Princeton University Press, 1944), 260–83; Hans Delbruck, *History of the Art of War, Volume I: Warfare in Antiquity*, translated by Walter J. Renfroe, Jr. (Lincoln, NE: University of Nebraska Press, 1990), first published in 1920.

[33] Delbruck 1990, 136.

[34] UN Charter:

> WE THE PEOPLES OF THE UNITED NATIONS DETERMINED … to **save succeeding generations from the scourge of war**, which twice in our lifetime has brought untold sorrow to mankind, … AND FOR THESE ENDS … to practice tolerance and live together in peace with one another as good neighbours, and to unite our strength to maintain international peace and security, and to ensure, by the acceptance of principles and the institution of methods, that armed force shall not be used, save in the common interest, and to employ international machinery for the promotion of the economic and social advancement of all peoples, CHAPTER I: PURPOSES AND PRINCIPLES: Article 1. The **Purposes of the United Nations** are: To **maintain international peace and security**, and to that end: to take effective collective measures for the **prevention and removal of threats to the peace**, and for **the suppression of acts of aggression or other breaches of the peace**, and to bring about by peaceful means, and in conformity with the principles of justice and international law, adjustment or settlement of international disputes or situations which might lead to a breach of the peace (emphasis added).

community embodied in the United Nations generated a new global societal narrative that included the rule of law to protect all states from existential threat. Firepower and maneuver were constrained to limited aims or internationally approved international bounds. Such constraints empower the value of narrative.

Every governing power seeks to connect its story to the existing societal narrative. Essentially, they seek to establish story-narrative resonance. Even the best and most effective government cannot perfectly make this connection. The gaps between the governing story and societal narrative or the weakening of story-narrative resonance are disruption. Successful narrative entrepreneurs seek to take advantage of the dissonance and expand that disruption and to then interpose their own story between the government story and the societal narrative.

Disruption happens through outside events and through the internal efforts of the narrative entrepreneurs. An external event can include natural disaster, invasion, or economic collapse as well as many other sources. Narrative entrepreneurs recognize the created disruption and then seek to expand it through their own efforts of engagement, media, and violence. As they do so, these actors are also trying to connect their story to the societal narrative.

As narrative entrepreneurs expand the governing story-narrative dissonance into disruption this may facilitate opportunities to displace the government's control of social functions and resources. Social functions are those things which all societies have and need: religion, security, transportation, health services, etc. Displacement can happen as disruption grows such that local people see that value of the narrative entrepreneur's story over that of the government. It also can happen as the narrative entrepreneur brings in additional resources from outside the conflict area. These outside resources may include foreign fighters.

The opening story of the 2014 battle of Mosul clearly shows the literal displacement of the Iraqi security forces as the disruption generated by ISIS created a sense of fear and intimidation in the minds of the security forces such that remaining at their posts was no longer a viable option—they needed to flee to guarantee safety. They needed to displace. ISIS was so effective as disruption that very little (relatively speaking) violence was needed to generate the desired displacement as tens of thousands of security force personnel either no longer reported to work or simply abandoned their posts. In effect, the months and years of effort prior to the actual battle on the part of ISIS created disruption over time that was cognitively exhausting such that when the precursors of the attacks began—the ISIS opponent displaced.

Narrative Shape/Structure as a Facilitator of Disruption[35]

Narrative is more than a word or a description for how people process information. The U.S. military likes to divide the environment of conflict into domains: space, air, land, sea, and cyberspace. Oddly enough, there is no attempt in the military doctrine to explain what a domain is.[36] A basic definition from the internet that provides a useful conceptualization is "a specified sphere of activity or knowledge."[37] This is a case where the etymology of the word is informative. The source word is French and means that which belongs to a lord. Following this logic, a conflict domain is an area over which a power wields controlling influence. For example, the sea domain is a domain because a naval power can wield controlling influence over it, or so the argument goes.

In this sense, one might question the U.S. military list of domains as at least a couple of them do not have, at the present and may never have, a controlling power.[38] For example, armies may control the land and navies might be able to control the sea, but it is debatable whether or not any force can control the air. It might be possible to control the air through a combination of electro-magnetic observation (radar), defensive systems (anti-aircraft missiles and guns), and aircraft. Who or what controls the internet or, more broadly, cyberspace? Can anything or anyone control space? Is it possible to do so through the same combination of tools as may be used to control the air?

Narrative may be a domain by this same reasoning. It is possible to control the narrative space as much as it is possible to control the land or sea. The term control may imply too much. A good army commander doesn't actually control the land. He typically controls the ability of the opponent to act on the land or the ability of his own army to gain a position of

---

35 Much of this section appeared earlier in Brian L. Steed, "Maneuvering within Islam's narrative space," *Strategic Review: The Indonesian Journal of Leadership, Policy and World Affairs* 8, no. 1 (January–March 2018): 16-35.

36 Jared Donnelly and Jon Farley, "Defining the 'Domain' in Multi-Domain," *Over the Horizon: Multi-Domain Operations & Strategy*, September 17, 2018.

37 *Lexico*, "Domain," accessed June 24, 2020, https://www.lexico.com/definition/domain.

38 United States Department of Defense, *DOD Dictionary of Military and Associated Terms,* United States Department of Defense, Washington DC, January 2020, 11, 55, 127, 136, 160, 198.

advantage on the land. That said, all of the same attendant challenges associated with controlling the land or sea are also present in controlling narrative in that it requires an understanding of the characteristics of the land, an understanding of what portions of the land provide relative advantage, and an appreciation of the enemy intent and desire for action on that land.

Figure 4: Geologic Metaphor of Narrative Space

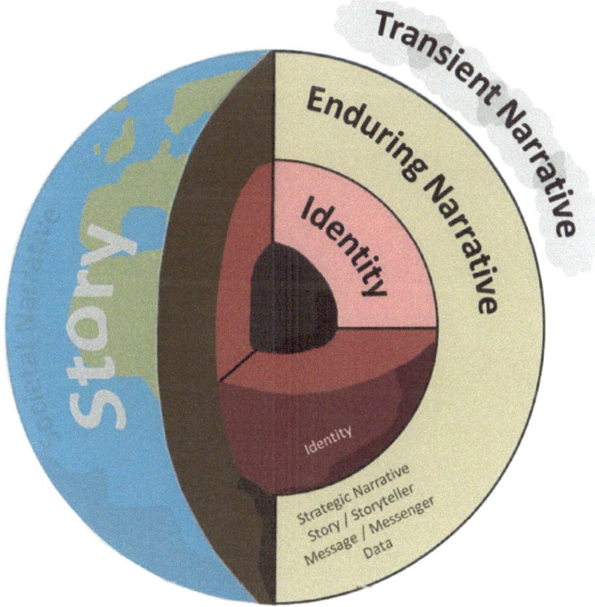

Narrative space has terrain, just as does physical space. Narrative space terrain is made up of ideas, concepts, humiliations, grievances, history, culture, language, religion, etc. that have different values in terms of shaping the thoughts, perceptions, and associated actions of people who reside in that narrative space. Narrative, for the purposes of this philosophical approach, includes social identity, enduring narrative and transient narrative. Figure 4 captures the imagery of this concept in the form of a geologic metaphor in that social identity forms the core of how the society or culture sees itself and the most deeply rooted narrative structures. It is the bedrock of the later described narrative space.

Enduring narrative is the crust that sits in between the core and the atmosphere of the transient narrative. It is the transition area between the daily narrative immersion and the core identity. Enduring narrative begins with the first instruction provided to a child. It includes customs, religion, culture, biases, mythology, prejudices, accepted truths and other formative-shaping means of filtering ideas and perceiving information.

It may be that every person has her own narrative; however, such an understanding is unworkable as no one can be expected to understand seven billion enduring narratives. The argument here is that the individual narratives coalesce into a collective or societal narrative that is comprehensible and the heart of this narrative domain.

Figure 5: Terrain Morphology Metaphor of Narrative Space

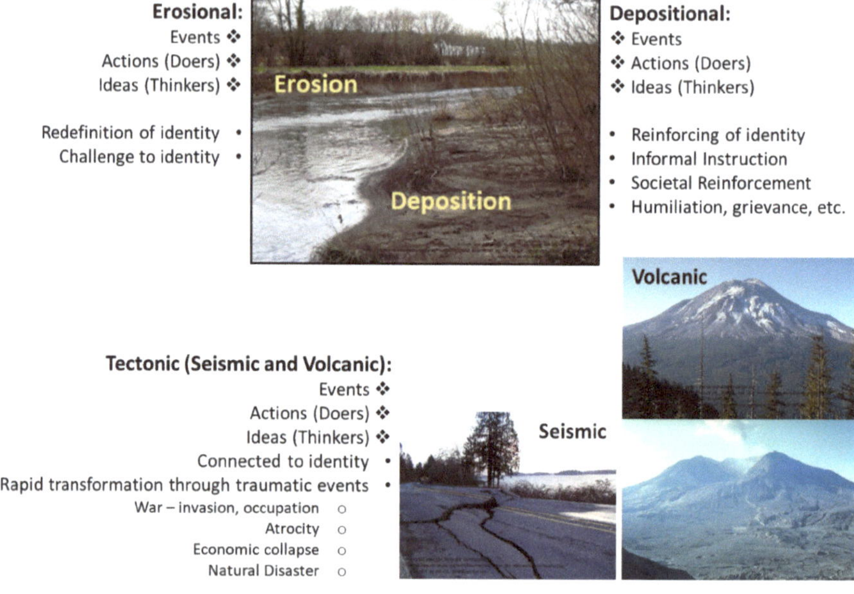

The enduring narrative is a constructed environment. Terrain, in the narrative space, is dynamic and may be altered by the "words-deeds-images" of any of the conflict participants.[39] In general, the terrain is primarily formed by the construct of societal identity and the enduring

[39] Matthew J. Yandura is quoted as saying "This is not a war for hearts and minds. This is a battle of words, deeds and images: We and our Afghan allies must win all three." Sohail Shaikh, "Narrative in the Operations Process: A case study: Voices of Moderate Islam" (presentation, October 23, 2017).

narrative. Identity-related terrain is the least likely to change, as this is created over generations and sometimes centuries of beliefs and common references and values. Enduring narrative and the terrain derived therefrom have a greater potential to change. Those conducting maneuver in the narrative space often seek to use the existing key and decisive terrain in this enduring narrative landscape to their advantage and may also seek to adjust that terrain through the transient narrative data/memes, messages, stories and the linked "words-deeds-images" associated with their maneuver.

Continuing with the geologic metaphor, narrative space terrain is constructed in much the same way as is physical terrain through basic processes of deposition, erosion and tectonic forces (see Figure 5), which creates a narrative landscape or narrative shape/structure. Understanding narrative shape and structure is narrative morphology. These processes, as with their physical counterparts, happen over long periods of time or can happen in violent episodic events. The primary shapers of this space are events, ideas (people-thinkers) and actions (people-doers).

Deposition is reinforcement of the preexisting narrative structure. This is an additive process that is building, sometimes for generations, the landscape. Every time a parent tells a child a story or points to a specific event with the same conceptual moral note that proves the story true that parent participates in a depositional event. Each subsequent event or story deposits a new layer of narrative sediment upon the preexisting landscape, reinforcing the shape/structure.

Erosion is changing the pre-existing narrative structure. As with deposition, this can occur over a long time, although this tends to be more episodic than does deposition. The comparison of deposition and erosion does not necessarily mean that deposition is good and erosion is bad. One is reinforcing and the other is changing. For example, when a child arrives at school for the first time, they may be challenged with new ideas, new social norms and different information than what they learned at home. All of this is erosional, as it reshapes interpretations of the world. This is a natural part of growth and development. However, depending on the nature of the erosional event, this can also be traumatic. Violent crime challenges personal safety. Religious missionaries can change definitions of salvation. Invasion, whether physical or cultural, can reshape values and aesthetics.

The final process is tectonic in that, like physical tectonic forces, it can be abrupt and significantly transformative in a single event. Also, like the physical counterpart, narrative tectonic events tend to work off generations of pre-existing stress that can be released in a single event. The single events are not transformative in and of themselves, but they are transformative, and sometimes radically so, because of the pre-existing conditions inclining the landscape toward change.

Figure 6: Interaction of Transient and Enduring Narrative

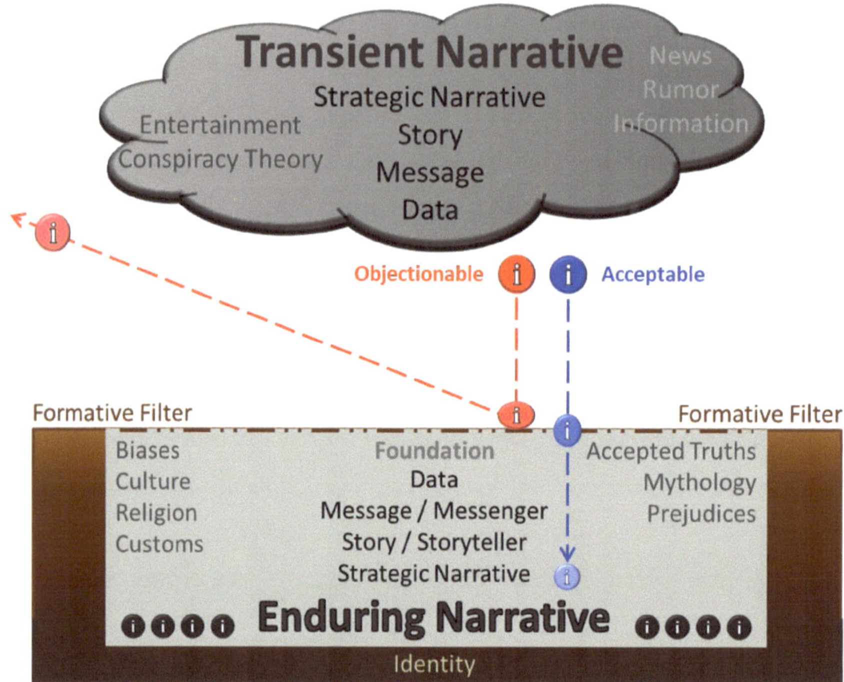

In each category, there are examples of people who are thinkers or doers who provide depositional, erosional or tectonic effects. There are also events, some natural and many man-made, that can provide the same variety of effects. The difference is in the speed of the effect. Depositional is the slowest and most consistent. Erosional can be either slow or fast, though it tends toward an opposingly similar consistent approach, as does depositional. The speed and drama of change comes from the tectonic people and events.

The transient narrative includes and may be closely analogous to the ever-changing and ubiquitous information environment. It includes news, rumor, information, entertainment, conspiracy theories and other time-sensitive means of information or data flow. The transient and the enduring narratives have inverse hierarchies of components. For the transient narrative, the highest is the strategic narrative and then the story, the message, and data or memes (see Figure 6).

The enduring narrative filters this hierarchy and reverses the order such that the first sorted are the data and memes and then the message, the story and finally the strategic narrative. The enduring narrative further filters messengers and storytellers for acceptability. This order expresses the ease with which elements may be able to pass through the filter as a meme or a piece of data is more likely to make it through the filter than is a fully formed story or strategic narrative.

When a person receives new information that has a potential impact on the narrative, that information is then filtered through the enduring narrative. Does it challenge or confirm the narrative? Based on the answer, and based on the individual's experience and the flexibility or permeability of the enduring narrative filter, the transient narrative information will either be accepted or rejected. If accepted, it may slightly adjust the narrative, and if rejected, it maintains the existing narrative's permanence—as described later, these are personal examples of depositional or erosional events. Transient narratives are accepted when they reinforce enduring narratives or identity. They are rejected when transient information challenges the enduring narratives or identity and are then seen as subversive. This leads to the information being discarded; sometimes as impure or sinful. This is not simply an issue of truth or fiction, but more importantly about concordant or discordant transient narratives.

The enduring narrative has terrain. Not every word or deed or image has the same efficacy or significance to the culture or the society. Some are more significant—in essence, there is high ground and there is low ground as created over time by the deposition, erosion, and tectonic forces. That makes it more difficult for any single governing story to connect tightly to the societal or enduring narrative—there are gaps. These gaps are disruptions. As there are few states with a single, homogenous societal narrative then the variance in the narratives within the state also further expand the instances of disruption. The following example illustrates these principles.

Example: The U.S. Created and Operationally Supported ISIS

An example of the interplay between transient and enduring narrative is evidenced in the fight against ISIS in Iraq. The most popular narrative in Iraq in early 2015, and continuing to 2016, was that the United States (and Israel) created and was (were) supporting ISIS in combat operations.[40] For the average American, this was ludicrous. The American identity and enduring narrative include concepts of freedom, justice, human rights, civil liberties, separation of church and state, and humanitarian behavior. What ISIS stands for, as popularly communicated in the U.S. media, runs counter to this American enduring narrative; thus, this transient narrative is discarded because the filter does not let it through. Because the transient narrative was rejected, there was no early counter from the US government in Iraq or beyond. It was simply deemed too ludicrous to comment on.[41] In Iraq, however, the narrative grew. Some say that the narrative started with the Iranians or other Shiite militia groups.[42] Regardless of where it started, by January 2015 everyone was saying it or thinking it—Arabs, Persians, Kurds, Shiites, Sunnis, Christians, Yazidis. It didn't matter who—they all were thinking it was true. Why?

A way to look at the Iraqi enduring narrative may go as follows: the United States hates Iraq. The average Iraqi in 1990 believed they were the pinnacle of Middle East might and civilization, and because of this Israel and the United States wanted to weaken and humiliate the great ancient power.[43] Starting in 1990, US forces began to harm their economy through sanctions. In 1991, the US-led military coalition destroyed much of the Iraqi infrastructure and security forces through Operation Desert Storm. From 1991 to 2003, the United States and its coalition allies imposed one of the harshest sanctions regimes ever leveled against a

---

[40] Joe Gould, "US-ISIS Rumors Hard to Counter, General Says," *Defense News*, May 21, 2015; Paul D. Shinkman, "Poll: Syrians, Iraqis Believe U.S. Created ISIS, Don't Support War," *US News*, December 18, 2015. Russia claimed on more than one occasion that the U.S. assisted ISIS in Syria. Shawn Snow, "Russia threatens US forces, calls America an obstacle to defeating ISIS in Syria," *Military Times*, October 4, 2017.

[41] Liz Sly, "Iraqis think the U.S. is in cahoots with the Islamic State, and it is hurting the war," *Washington Post*, December 1, 2015.

[42] Brian L. Steed, Unpublished Personal Journal of Events as the Chief of Engagements for the Deputy Commanding General-Advising and Training, United States Forces-Iraq, Baghdad, Iraq, 2011.

[43] Anthony Shadid, *Night Draws Near: Iraq's People in the Shadow of America's War* (New York: Henry Holt and Company, 2005), 35–39.

country, dramatically harming not just the economy but all of Iraqi society.[44] In 2003, President George W. Bush continued what his father George H.W. Bush began by invading the country and destroying the government; throwing the country into chaos. Then after eight years of occupation, instability, and mayhem and just as things appeared to be stabilizing, the United States withdrew, creating another round of confusion and turmoil.[45] Just as the prime minister was getting his hands on the problems, which a Sunni would say were the necks of the Sunnis, in comes ISIS to create more catastrophe.

Americans may say this doesn't make sense because we were providing support for the Iraqi government. Why would the United States support both? The Iraqi enduring narrative about America includes U.S. Congressional testimony in 1987 where it was revealed that the American government sold arms and equipment to both Iraq and Iran at the same time during the Iran-Iraq War as part of the Iran-Contra affair. Therefore, the United States has a history of double-dealing when it comes to Iraq. When one sees images of ISIS fighters, they are typically wearing American made gear (or something similar to it) and driving U.S.-made vehicles. The United States must be equipping them. This is photographic evidence of support to ISIS. American officials say that ISIS got this equipment when they captured it from Iraqi security forces. Most Iraqis do not know that the U.S. government sold or gave so much equipment to the Iraqi Security Forces.[46] There are videos showing Iraqi soldiers or militia members holding up American meals-ready-to-eat, or MREs, that they say they found in ISIS positions.[47] This will be excused by saying the MREs may have come from airdropped pallets blown off course and intended for the Yazidis on Mount Sinjar or Kurdish fighters in northern Iraq. When Tikrit was retaken in May 2015, *The New York Times* interviewed a Shiite militia fighter who said he saw the United States support ISIS fighters during the battle with his own eyes.[48]

Iraqis glean further support for their narrative from political speeches such as those

---

[44] Shadid, *Night Draws Near*, 35–39.

[45] Joel Rayburn, *Iraq After America: Strongmen, Sectarians, Resistance* (Stanford, CA: Hoover Institution Press, 2014), 243.

[46] Steed, Unpublished Personal Journal of Events as the Chief of Engagements for the Deputy Commanding General-Advising and Training, United States Forces-Iraq, Baghdad, Iraq, 2011.

[47] Sly, "Iraqis think the U.S. is in cahoots with the Islamic State, and it is hurting the war," *Washington Post*, December 1, 2015.

[48] Rod Nordland, "Iraq Forces, Pushing ISIS Out of Tikrit, Give Few Thanks for U.S. Air Strikes," *The New York Times*, April 2, 2015.

made during the 2016 U.S. presidential primary and general election campaigns. Democratic candidates said that the Islamic State was created through the actions of George W. Bush and the invasion and occupation of Iraq (2003-2011). In contrast, Republican candidates and pundits on the right blamed the creation of the Islamic State on the withdrawal of U.S. forces from Iraq in 2011 by President Barack Obama.[49] In either case, all sides of the American political spectrum feed into the narrative that the United States, one way or the other, created ISIS.

In sum, the enduring Iraqi narrative is that the United States and its coalition allies have a singular purpose of making the people of Iraq suffer. Additionally, the United States wants to protect Israel, and keeping Iraq weak and divided by Shiite and Sunni killing each other serves that purpose. Furthermore, the Iraqi people have seen what the United States does when it is serious about a problem: it deploys tens of thousands of forces and mountains of gear and material. That is not what the United States did in the fight against ISIS. The United States, through its technology, can control all of its actions and sees and knows what is happening throughout Iraq—or so the narrative goes—and thus nothing happens by accident.[50] Therefore, if bad things happen, the United States knows it and can do something about it, if so desired. Because ISIS continued to exist for years after President Obama called for its destruction, then the United States must not want to defeat the group as it claimed.

Narrative Space: Holistic Understanding

Narrative space is not truly a separate space despite the depiction in Figure 7; rather, it includes cyberspace and physical space as they are all interrelated. The figure shows narrative space separate to communicate that it is a domain that requires a different way of thinking. Narrative space terrain preexists maneuver by any party in the conflict and denotes the inherent value within the community in which the competitors seek to attain a position of advantage. In effect, narrative determines what has value in the sense of what is the high ground and what are the

---

[49] Susan Milligan, "After Paris Attacks, Democratic Candidates Blame Bush for ISIS," *US News and World Report*, 14 November 14, 2015; Michael Crowley, "Who Lost Iraq? Did George W. Bush create the Islamic State? Did Barack Obama? We asked the insiders to tell us who's to blame." *Politico Magazine*, July/August 2015; Jon Austin, "'CIA created ISIS', says Julian Assange as Wikileaks releases 500k US cables," *Express UK*, 29 November 29, 2016.

[50] Emma Sky, *The Unraveling: High Hopes and Missed Opportunities in Iraq* (New York: Public Affairs, 2015), 35.

resources worthy of conflict. Terrain, in the narrative space, is dynamic and nonlinear as it may be altered by the words-deeds-images of any of the conflict participants.

Figure 7: Narrative Space: Holistic Representation

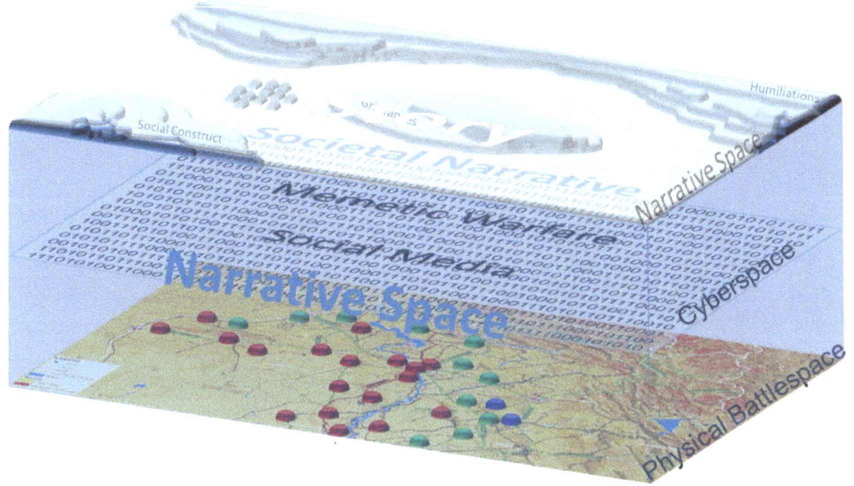

In summing up this discussion on the construct of narrative, this is about the way humans process information and make decisions. The stories are the real world and they matter. The structure and organization of stories is based off the narrative shape/structure that gives shape to the stories and also provides purpose and direction to the characters in those stories. As noted in the figure where the story seems to sit nicely if imperfectly on the societal narrative, this story will always have some gap between it and the societal narrative. No governing story will perfectly adhere. The dissonance between story and societal narrative is the disruption that narrative entrepreneurs seek to expand into displacement.

Figure 8: Geologic Metaphor Demonstrating Disruption Becoming Displacement

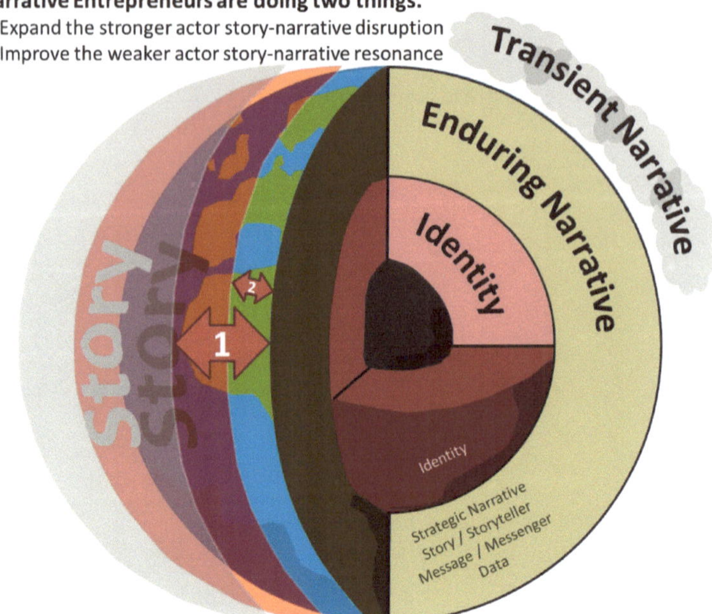

The Position of Advantage Provides the Place and Power for Displacement

The narrative entrepreneur seeks to expand the separation between the governing power's story and the societal narrative while at the same time communicating clearly that its story more fully matches the societal narrative (see Figure 8). The successful narrative entrepreneur does this by controlling narrative high ground or using a narrative position of advantage. The U.S. Army places some emphasis and effort on defining and explaining a position of relative advantage in its key doctrinal manual called simply *Operations*. The use of the modifying term relative is important as conflict is regularly characterized as a dyadic event and therefore everything so described should be viewed in relation to an opposing party:

> A position of relative advantage is a location or the establishment of a favorable condition within the area of operations that provides the commander with temporary freedom of action to enhance combat power over an enemy or influence the enemy to accept risk and move to a position of disadvantage. Positions of relative advantage occur in all domains, providing opportunities for

> units to exploit. … A key aspect in achieving a position of advantage is maneuver, the employment of forces in the operational area through movement in combination with fires to achieve a position of advantage in respect to the enemy.
>
> Positions of relative advantage are usually temporary and require initiative to exploit. While friendly forces are seeking positions of advantage, enemy forces are doing the same. There are multiple forms of positional advantage that provide opportunities to exploit. … Examples of positional advantage include—
>
> - Legitimacy, ideas, and popular perception (including what is good versus bad, accepted versus opposed, and a believable narrative).
> - Moral (including alignment of words and deeds, just and unjust, and international support).
> - Will (including doing what must be done, continuing as long as it takes, and maintaining support from domestic leaders).[51]

Maneuver is the combination of movement and fires. For the sake of narrative war, fires may be a combination of violence, social media, and historical and contextual understanding or words-deeds-images. Such an appreciation was shown through the attack on the al-Askari Shrine in Samarra, Iraq in 2006.[52] To appreciate the targeting of this shrine it is important to recognize the narrative significance of the shrine. The shrine is named for Ali al-Hadi and his son Hasan al-Askari who are known as the two Askaris and who are revered by those who adhere to Twelver Shia as the 10th and 11th Imams. The 12th Imam, for whom the sect is named, is believed to have gone into occultation from this location and that he will return from occultation in the end days to this shrine. So, this shrine is really the source of the name of the largest sub-group of Shia and is also deeply connected to the eschatology of that sect. There are few other shrines in Shia Islam that are equally significant. The ability to harm such a place is attacking a narrative position of relative advantage.

The bombing of the Al Askari Shrine, on 22 February 2006, initiated a bloody civil war between Sunni and Shiite throughout Iraq, but primarily in Baghdad. Prior to the U.S. invasion and the insurgency that rose in opposition to it, Iraq was relatively nonsectarian and certainly did not include the torture and slaughter of members of other sects by private citizens—torture

---

[51] United States Department of the Army, *FM 3-0: Operations*. Headquarters, United States Department of the Army, Washington DC, October 6, 2017, 1-18–1-19. The examples are edited to show those most closely connected to narrative.

[52] Joel D. Rayburn, Frank K. Sobchak, Jeanne F. Godfroy, Matthew D. Morton, James S. Powell, and Matthew M. Zais, editors, *The U.S. Army in the Iraq War — Volume 1: Invasion, Insurgency, and Civil War, 2003-2006,* (Carlisle Barracks, PA: Strategic Studies Institute and U.S. Army War College Press, January 2019), 342, 532–33.

was reserved for Saddam's regime. Many Iraqis were married across sectarian lines and most Iraqi tribes included families from both Sunni and Shiite sects. The transformation of this stable environment to one of bloody sectarian violence took only a matter of months. Comments by Iraqis in 2016 that they could not trust members of other sects as ISIS governed large portions of the country were relatively new and unique in Iraqi history.[53] Iraqis had not been killing each other for hundreds or thousands of years. This sectarian murder started in 2003 and grew rapidly over time due to words-deeds-images in the narrative space that both erupted and shook the existing societal norms, eroded old nonsectarian attitudes and then deposited notions of fear and loathing, sowing distrust between the communities. This all happened within months and years. Narrative space terrain can change and evolve rapidly. Iraq provides a sad example of such transformation.

From 2006 to 2011, the U.S. government, through investment of personnel, equipment and money, also changed the Iraqi security forces and the trust with the populace for the better. The events and attitudes associated with the "surge" are an example of positive change through hard work to first erode the negative narrative landscape and then deposit along favorable lines for the United States, coalition forces, and Iraqi security forces. Although there are critics of this example, it is difficult to argue that violence was not reduced and trust not increased between the Iraqi people and their security forces.[54] Narrative terrain can be shaped and changed by both indigenous and foreign thinkers, doers and events. And it doesn't always take decades.

This transformation was made possible over such a short period of time because of the ability to identify and use relative positions of advantage within the narrative space. ISIS used a characterization of the U.S. as a Roman crusader because those were terms that resonated with the Iraqi societal narrative of an oppressive power against Muslims that existed in the past and one that was prophesied to conduct operations in the end of days. The overthrow of

---

[53] Associated Press, "10 Years on, Iraq Scarred from Attack on Shiite Shrine," *The New York Times*, February 21, 2016; Rayburn, et al. *The U.S. Army in the Iraq War — Volume 1,* January 2019, 533–39.

[54] Peter Mansoor, *Surge: My Journey with General David Petraeus and the Remaking of the Iraq War* (New Haven, CT: Yale University Press, 2013); Carter Malkasian, *Illusions of Victory: The Anbar Awakening and the Rise of the Islamic State* (New York: Oxford University Press, 2017); Joel D. Rayburn et al., editors, *The U.S. Army in the Iraq War—Volume 2: Surge and Withdrawal, 2007-2011.*

Saddam Hussein and the chaos that followed was spun throughout the Islamic world as a sign of the end of days and the rapidly approaching battle to be fought at Dabiq (or Amaq).[55] This was the apocalyptic battle where the army of the righteous would fight the Roman-crusaders and be led to victory by Jesus. The locations, the events, the opposing powers fit within the societal narrative.

Relative positions of advantage within the narrative space matter.

Displacement: America 2020

I have been reticent to bring up the events of the late Spring and Summer of 2020 as I want to avoid politization of these ideas; however, the events as part of the COVID-19 pandemic and the American protests and riots provide fantastic examples of these same concepts. In effect, America had, as do all large and heterogenous countries, multiple societal narratives. One of those narratives was encapsulated in *The New York Times Magazine* "1619 Project" that was first published in August 2019. The most extreme assertion of that project was that America was founded on slavery and racism. This narrative runs counter to the more generally accepted narrative prominent since the 1960s that the United States was founded on idealist principles that have yet to be fully realized.[56] One narrative expresses a positive and aspirational American dream and the other expresses that the United States system has been, from its conception, tainted by foundational problems of racism. The death of George Floyd while under police authority in Minneapolis, Minnesota on 25 May 2020 generated a variety of stories concerning the use or abuse of police authority, the failure of the government to meet the needs of citizens, and the role of race in both. The words and phrases used connected the various stories to the competing societal narratives and served to separate groups or displace authority from dealing with those who defaced or damaged public property. Individuals and groups protested and some attacked buildings and statues as symbols that were relative positions of advantage—government facilities; police and police precincts; and statues of

[55] Dabiq, 2014, "The Return of the Khalifah," *Dabiq*, issue 1, Islamic State [5 July 2014], 2, 4-5.

[56] The prominent American narrative prior to the 1960s essentially ignored those who had been left out of the benefits of the American dream. Starting with the new history introduced in the middle of the 20th century in American colleges and universities, there was greater and greater emphasis placed on the voices in America not represented in scholarship and popular discourse.

presidents, generals, Confederate leaders, etc.

Almost everyone agreed that what happened to George Floyd was a miscarriage of justice. However, the acts observed and reported by many rapidly moved away from points of narrative agreement toward symbols and positions of relative advantage that were more extreme and that served to displace authority. The existence of the Capitol Hill Autonomous Zone (later named the Capitol Hill Occupied Protest and the Capitol Hill Organized Protest) that existed across several blocks of downtown Seattle, Washington from 8 June to 1 July 2020 was one of the most extreme examples of displacement. The people who established this zone supposedly outside local, state, and federal government authority used the disruption in the government story-narrative resonance to expand that to literal and physical displacement of police and government authority and services from the area.

In these American events, the conduct of maneuver in the narrative space is clear as the hierarchy of narrative structures exist in the form of memes, messages, stories, strategic narratives, and societal narratives clashed. Different people saw the same things and interpreted those things in radically different ways. Almost all Americans viewed the death of George Floyd while under police authority as heinous. Because of the narrative of some, this act demanded protest. Some believed it demanded revolution. Some believed it demanded reform and retraining of police. The societal narrative accepted by any given person drove what stories were accepted, what memes inspired action, and what messages to spread by that person. The recorded and broadcast death of an African American man served as a powerful, destructive, and transformational relative position of advantage.

Displacement: The Deceptive Media Halo

In the book, *The Management of Savagery: The Most Critical Stage Through Which the Umma Will Pass*, written under the pseudonym Abu Bakr Naji in 2004, the community of believers of Islam and those willing to fight for Islam for whom the book was written are warned against the power of the deceptive media halo of the Russians and the Americans.[57] The term deceptive

---

[57] Abu Bakr Naji, *The Management of Savagery: The Most Critical Stage Through Which the Umma Will Pass*, translated by William McCants (Cambridge, MA: John M. Olin Institute for Strategic Studies, 23 May 2006), written in 2004. There are multiple references to the deceptive media halo that begin in the introduction. The most significant discussion happens in pages 17–19.

media halo is a fascinatingly poetic and artistic term. I recommend that a reader consider the halos of Renaissance art and the purpose of that halo. Halos were typically painted around the head or around the body of saints or holy figures so that the viewer of the art clearly understood who was being represented in the artwork. In contemporary sense this halo represents holiness or purity. In a more relevant sense to the artists painting the work and to Abu Bakr Naji, the halo represented power. Yes, it denoted purity and holiness. That purity and holiness served as a connection to God. Connection to God affords power and ability to accomplish one's objectives as expressed by Naji:

> There is no doubt that the power which God gave to the two superpowers (America and Russia) was overwhelming in the estimation of humans. However, in reality and after careful reflection using pure, human reason, (one comes to understand that this power) is not able to impose its authority from the country of the center—from America, for example, or Russia—upon lands in Egypt and Yemen, for example, unless these (latter) countries submit to those powers entirely of their own accord. It is correct that this power is overwhelming and that it seeks help from the power of local regimes controlled by proxies [*al-wukalā'*] who rule the Islamic world. Yet all of that is not enough (to completely control the satellite states). Therefore, the two superpowers must resort to using a deceptive media halo which portrays these powers as non-coercive and world-encompassing, able to reach into every earth and heaven as if they possess the power of the Creator of creation.
>
> But the interesting thing that happened is that these two superpowers believed, for a time, their media deception: that they are actually a power capable of completely controlling any place in the entire world, and that (this power) bears the characteristics of the power of the Creator. According to the media deception, it is an all-encompassing, overwhelming power and people are subservient to it not only through fear, but also through love because it spreads freedom, justice, equality among humanity, and various other slogans.[58]

The reason that Abu Bakr Naji uses the adjective deceptive in his description of the media halo is that he is expressing that Russia and America are not pure and holy. They do not have connection to God. They are not filled with the power of God. It is the media that generates this false halo effect as it shows the powerful and technologically advanced countries as being better because of their material wealth and their, from Naji's perspective,

[58] Naji, *The Management of Savagery*, 17–18.

false claims of support for concepts of human rights and justice. Naji recognizes that this deceptive media halo affords the opponents of al-Qaeda a position of relative advantage—the object of maneuver.[59]

Hence, it is incumbent on those fighting such powers that they displace them from this position of relative advantage so that the contest is waged more appropriate to the Islamists. From Naji's perspective, his narrative is naturally superior. It is imbued with power because it comes from and is directly connected to God.

Narrative war is not necessarily won through control of hilltops or river crossings. It is won by controlling the narrative space in the form of the social functions: the shrines, symbols, and temples that dominate the societal narrative. One does not need to control everything, just what matters. In an overly simplified explanation, Napoleon could defeat a superior force using the maneuver philosophy of war by defeating the right part of the enemy which led to the disintegration of the enemy army and victory. The firepower philosophy led to a more attritional approach to war –the destruction of large portions of the opposing military and infrastructure—such that the enemy could not sustain war. Narrative war does not need to displace the opponent from every federal building or remove every statue or capture every city. ISIS caused displacement of a massive security force from Mosul because it generated a sense of power and commitment that communicated a capability much greater than reality. It worked and it took the city.[60]

Exhaustion is the Success Mechanism (Strategy)

How do you plan to win? What is your strategy? I have asked dozens, maybe hundreds, of students this question over the years that I have taught in professional military education. The response is often confusion. The confused students do not know what I mean. This is, in part, because they have been taught that strategy is fundamentally an accounting or bookkeeping exercise—a balancing of ends, ways, and means. It is about making sure that the withdrawals

---

[59] I reference al-Qaeda because Naji, by all accounts was a representative scholar and strategic philosopher for al-Qaeda when he wrote this; however, this book was very popular among ISIS fighters and leaders and serves as a great tool to explain the ISIS approach to fighting. See Alastair Crooke, 2014, "The ISIS' 'Management of Savagery' in Iraq," *The World Post*, June 30, 2014; Weis and Hassan, *ISIS: Inside the Army of Terror*, 44–46.

[60] Singer and Brooking, *Like War: The Weaponization of Social Media*.

associated with the desired endstate or the ends of the problem are matched up with the deposits of the associated resources needed and available to accomplish the ends. These resources are the means. The final part is the method or way to accomplish the endstate. Because, in the U.S. military we have already accepted that the right way is a way of firepower or targeting then there isn't much discussion on the methodology.

Strategy might be about making sure that the ends, ways, and means are appropriately in line with each other; however, the methodology should be open for question. A simple way to look at the available methods comes from Antulio J. Echevarria II's book *Military Strategy: A Very Short Introduction*. He offers ten strategies for fighting a war and he provides them in five couplets.[61] One of his five couplets is attrition and exhaustion. There is a lot more that could be said about strategy, but Echevarria, in combination with Delbruck, provides enough to say that exhaustion is the active strategy for narrative war.

Abu Bakr Naji illuminates the problems faced by any weaker power as it fights a stronger power. He says that there are three elements of the stronger power: centralization, overwhelming military power, and the deceptive media halo.[62] These three reside in a cohesive story. As weaker powers look at the U.S., as Naji explains, they see a large, powerfully controlled central authority, but with a variety of competing sub-groups. The only thing that centralizes the competing groups is a cohesive story. That story must be attacked and forced to lose coherence. Naji provides a level of detail as he expands on this concept:

> What if this assisting element is the decree of God which He ordained in order to act upon these three axes? It would not only work to activate the latent elements of cultural annihilation but confront the military power with **exhaustion**. This confrontation and **exhaustion** directly affects the third axis, which is the deceptive media halo. It removes the aura of invincibility which this power projects, that nothing at all stands in front of it.
>
> This is exactly what happened to the Communist superpower when it was put in a military confrontation with a power weaker than itself by several degrees;

---

[61] Antulio J. Echevarria II, *Military Strategy: A Very Short Introduction* (New York: Oxford University Press, 2017. The couplets are:

1. Annihilation and dislocation
2. Attrition and exhaustion
3. Deterrence and coercion
4. Terror and terrorism
5. Decapitation and targeted killing

[62] Naji, *The Management of Savagery*, 19.

it was not even comparable. However, (the weaker power) succeeded in **exhausting** it militarily and, even more important, it activated the elements of cultural annihilation in (the superpower's) homeland:

- The dogma of atheism versus belief systems that believe in the next life and a God.
- Love of the world, worldly pleasures, and opulence versus individuals who had nothing to lose.
- Moral corruption, the least manifestation of which was that Russian soldiers or officers returned (home)—if they returned—and found that their wives had a child or relationship with someone else.
- Social iniquities clearly floated to the surface when the economic situation weakened because of the war. Then when money becomes scarce and monetary crises begin, the major thieves appear, especially if accurate accounting [?] begins.

Additionally, note that the economic weakness resulting from the burdens of war or from aiming blows of vexation (al-nikāya) directly toward the economy is the **most important element of cultural annihilation** since it threatens the opulence and (worldly) pleasures which those societies thirst for. Then competition for these things begins after they **grow scarce due to the weakness of the economy**. Likewise, social iniquities rise to the surface on account of the economic stagnation, which ignites political opposition and disunity among the (various) sectors of society [literally "social entity"] in the central country (emphasis added).[63]

Abu Bakr Naji's assertions express the plan for defeating the super powers. One, they are without the power of God. Two, the population important to the Muslims and the population important to the super power are deceived by the media halo that surrounds the super power and imbues it with powers in the eyes of the people. Three, the way to defeat this super power is to stay in the fight regardless of the immediate results. Remaining in the fight allows for exhaustion to occur. Exhaustion, in the expression of Abu Bakr Naji, is the way to defeat the media halo. The previous quote, given in some length, allows for a reader to understand the supporting logic applied. The mujahidin that defeated the Soviet Union in Afghanistan between 1979 and 1989 did so because they stayed in the fight and revealed, over time, the moral weakness of the Soviet Union leading to its ultimate collapse. I expect that ISIS and other like-minded thinkers will be saying in 2020 that the same is true of America as

---

[63] Naji, *The Management of Savagery*, 19–20.

it admitted defeat by cutting a deal with the Taliban in early 2020 only to have America torn apart with political dissent and division later that same year.

The following paragraph from Naji in combination with the last paragraph of the preceding quote provide insight into the total vision of this program. The defeat mechanism of exhaustion is not to be provided by the direct actions of the mujahidin themselves. Rather, the exhaustion comes from a third order effect. The first action is that the mujahidin attack a type of target. The first order effect is that the powerful actor responds to that attack. The second order effect is that the powerful actor and its allies fortify similar types of targets expended resources in the form of manpower, salaries, infrastructure improvements, technology, etc. All of these improvements cost lots of money. The third order effect is the economic drag and eventual collapse of the powerful states under the economic weight of their actions to defend against future attacks:

> Diversify and widen the vexation strikes against the Crusader-Zionist enemy in every place in the Islamic world, and even outside of it if possible, so as to disperse the efforts of the alliance of the enemy and thus drain it to the greatest extent possible. For example: If a tourist resort that the Crusaders patronize in Indonesia is hit, all of the tourist resorts in all of the states of the world will have to be **secured by the work of additional forces**, which are double the ordinary amount, and a **huge increase in spending**. If a usurious bank belonging to the Crusaders is struck in Turkey, all of the banks belonging to the Crusaders will have to be **secured in all of the countries** and the (economic) **draining will increase**. If an oil interest is hit near the port of Aden, there will have to be **intensive security measures put in place for all of the oil companies**, and their tankers, and the oil pipelines in order to protect them and **draining will increase**. If two of the apostate authors are killed in a simultaneous operation in two different countries, they will have to secure thousands of writers in other Islamic countries. In this way, there is a diversification and widening of the circle of targets and vexation strikes which are accomplished by small, separate groups. Moreover, repeatedly (striking) the same kind of target two or three times will make it clear to them that this kind (of target) will continue to be vulnerable.
>
> ... Hitting economic targets will force (the enemy) to goad the regimes, who are (already) exhausted from protecting the other remaining targets (economic or otherwise), into pumping in more forces for its protection. **As a result, feebleness will start to appear in their forces**, especially since their forces are limited, for there is a rule for the regimes of apostasy that says: police

forces and the army in general, and the forces.[64]

The key to exhaustion is that this is economic exhaustion rather than direct military or security exhaustion. This is a long game. As America pulls out of Iraq and Afghanistan and other countries throughout the Middle East and other parts of the world, it dispels the deceptive media halo. America's own actions, so the argument goes, are proof of the proposition that America is not all-powerful. Again, international news coverage of Americans tearing their own cities apart serves to provide support to this extremist story of success. This empowers people to stay in the fight and concomitantly drags out the fighting and defensive measures such that they collapse the economies of all those in opposition to the mujahidin.

This expression of exhaustion may be directly connected to the actions of a specific type of actor; however, one can observe similar behaviors demonstrated in different actors across the globe: state and non-state alike. North Korea, Iran, China, and Russia all seek to play long games that are consistent drains on the American economy while also conducting a variety of attacks that either generate, encourage, or magnify unrest in America or attack and weaken the faith in the American political process. If America, or the West more broadly, is focused on problems at home then it won't be willing or able to conduct freedom of navigation exercises, have the consensus to deter nuclear proliferation, or to oppose arguably insignificant territorial expansion.

Solutions

This section is short as the answer to the question—what kind of solutions are there?—is best answered with, it depends. The things on which such an answer depends includes the audience, the purpose of the weaker organization, the intent of the stronger actor action, and many others. Some general thoughts are still informative.

It all starts with narrative morphology. This is the study and understanding of the shape/structure of narrative space. Several key parts of narrative morphology follow. First, story-narrative resonance is a thing and it needs to be recognized and understood. Below are some questions that address how one can look at the dynamics in a specific country with which

---

[64] Naji, *The Management of Savagery*, 46, 47.

a stronger actor is or will interact:

- What is the societal narrative?
- What is the governing coalition story?
- What generated the disruption in the story-narrative resonance?
- Is the disruption increasing or reducing?
- Is the governing story desirable?
- If no, can it be reasonably changed and maintain governance?
- How can the intervening stronger actor positively affect the story-narrative resonance?
- What is the weaker actor story?
- Why is that story resonating with the societal narrative?
- How can the intervening stronger actor negatively affect the story-narrative resonance?

Second, significant disruption leads to displacement. The point at which disruption turns to displacement can vary wildly. For example, Hezbollah versus the Israeli occupation of southern Lebanon, U.S. operations in Afghanistan, and ISIS in Iraq involved the intervention of some level of foreign entity that created the displacement of local governance when each intervened. How did disruption lead to displacement in the Russian invasion and takeover of Crimea? At what point will China's disruptive conduct globally and in the South China Sea displace the U.S. Navy and other international actors from asserting basic norms of behavior? It is important to develop greater understanding of when disruption facilitates displacement and whether or not it is consistent. Foreign invasion or intervention is an obvious point of displacement as the government is literally no longer in control of an area of its own country. The cases previously mentioned also give examples of non-invasion displacement through consistent government failure to deliver on the basic expectations of citizens extant from the societal narrative. For example, Lebanon did not provide social services to the Shia, the Hamid Karzai government could not provide sufficient security forces nor could it control the Americans operating in Afghanistan, and Nuri al-Maliki persecuted Sunni Iraqis to the point that they no longer felt a part of Iraq. Such disruptions easily facilitated moves toward displacement. One point of note is that fractured governments seem to be easier to displace than would be a unified government. Hezbollah, the Taliban, and ISIS have all been harder to remove than were the governments that those actors displaced.

Third, exhaustion comes as resilience weakens. Resilient societies have stories, and probably master narratives, that include overcoming adversity. It is built in that the society deals with hard times and maybe existential threats and continues to rebuild and improve. Most long-lasting societies have such master narratives and stories or the society wouldn't have survived for centuries.

Conclusion

You know that you never defeated us on the battlefield," said the American colonel. The North Vietnamese colonel pondered this remark for a moment. "That may be so," he replied, "but it is also irrelevant.[65]

— Harry J. Summers

Military professionals have often placed greater emphasis on violence than on narrative. After all, violence is what the military does. Since the military is the primary national instrument involved in conflict, it seems natural that the emphasis in preparation for and during conflicts would be on violence. Each practitioner of narrative war uses and used violence. In almost all cases, they used a lot of violence. The point is that such groups are or were successful because of their understanding and use of narrative and not their use of violence. The quote above addresses that reality. The U.S. war in Vietnam involved a tremendous amount of violence on both sides; however, the ultimate victor was not the actor that provided the most violence or even had the most success in the violence competition. It was the actor who best recognized and best used narrative.

A recent example of this expression happened on 29 February 2020, when the United

[65] Harry G. Summers, Jr., *On Strategy: A Critical Analysis of the Vietnam War* (Novato, CA: Presidio Press, 1982), 1.

States of America signed an agreement with the Taliban of Afghanistan that allowed the Taliban to participate in the governance process in Afghanistan and indicated that the U.S. would withdraw from the country as a fighting force after a year and a half. The details of the agreement are not particularly crucial, but the overall concept is critical. It is difficult to imagine the U.S. negotiating directly with the Taliban along these lines fifteen years earlier. The fact that these negotiations occurred and that an agreement was reached without the participation of the government of Afghanistan further speaks to the effectiveness of the philosophy outlined in this chapter. The Taliban disrupted the government of Afghanistan and its American allies until it was invited to a seat at the table. It effectively displaced the government of Afghanistan such that government representatives weren't allowed to be present as the fate of Afghanistan was negotiated. Despite numerous stops and starts, the Taliban was able to get the U.S. to agree to Taliban participation in the governance of Afghanistan because American presidents have become exhausted with a war that seems to never end.

The seeming failure in Afghanistan—after nearly twenty years of conflict only to return to power those who were ousted at the beginning—in combination with a similar perception of Iraq—defeat one insurgency only to leave and allow in another—has generated a sense of frustration with American technological power. The U.S. has the ability to physically dominate, but not the ability to win. Winning is when one side concedes desired interests or influence to the other. In concrete terms, winning for a weaker actor is obtaining governance over territory. Why can't the U.S. win as often or as quickly or as decisively as desired if it enjoys such an overwhelming advantage in raw destructive power?

Summary of the Argument

This chapter offered a unique and important approach to answering this question. Weaker actors understand the value of three conditions: understanding of the actual conflict environment at the local level, generation of support through a story that provides a believable path to victory, and consistency sufficient to generate support over time. Furthermore, weaker actors use a better and more detailed understanding of narrative to recognize pre-existing narrative disruptions. The weaker actor then expands the disruptions by actions of its own. As disruption expands, the weaker actor has greater opportunity and ability to displace stronger actor governance across a wide spectrum of social functions. Disruption and displacement are not entirely sequential. They overlap and, at times, occur simultaneously. The displacement, at its extreme, has a weaker actor behaving as the government.

Displacement occurs in situations where disruption is growing. It is caused, in part, by the perception that the weaker power (usually a non-state actor, though not always) is on the side of the people, whereas the government no longer is, if it ever had been. Under such conditions, people are inclined to side with the people like them. This isn't a benign and peaceful endeavor. This process occurs with violence; however, violence is less necessary when the weaker actor offers a story closer to the societal narrative than that of the stronger actor. Conflict is both Darwinian and utilitarian: "If you can persuade a person, you don't need to kill him."[66]

Not all weaker actors seek to fully displace the governance of the stronger actor at first. It may only be disruption and partial displacement that is sought, as the weaker actor may recognize that it does not currently possess the ability to provide the social functions or resources the community needs to maintain positive control.

All of this occurs within a strategy of exhaustion—wearing down the will of the opponent. Hans Delbruck phrased one of his two types of strategies as fatigue strategy.[67] When members of the village or town government are fatigued by constant attacks and a perception of a never-ending war, they may be inclined to turn toward the weaker and seemingly ever present and ever active actor. This sentiment is best articulated by Ho Chi Minh when he stated to a French official, "You can kill ten of my men for every one I kill of yours. But even at those odds, you will lose and I will win."[68] The weaker actor communicates with its understanding of narrative that it cannot be defeated and by so doing, it exhausts the stronger actor.

Most conflicts since World War II end in something other than a stronger actor win,

---

[66] Timothy B. Lawn, 2019, "Narrative Landmines and Combatting Foreign Influence," *Narrative Strategies Journal*, Issue 2 (January 24, 2019): 15.
[67] Delbruck, *History of the Art of War,* 136.

[68] Stanley Karnow, *Vietnam: A History* (New York: The Viking Press, 1983), 183.

and as often as the stronger actor wins, conflicts tend to end in something that can't be defined as a win or loss. Many of the conflicts turn in to some other type of conflict with a different set of opponents or across another border. Such conceptualization of conflict that transforms rather than concludes leads to an exhausting perception of unending war. The Vietnam War for the U.S. is such an example. Those who would become the North Vietnamese and Viet Cong had previously been Viet Minh fighting against the French or ethnic Vietnamese fighting against the Japanese. By the time Saigon fell to Hanoi some form of war had been going on in that area for more than thirty years. Afghanistan is a similar example. The Taliban today were mujahidin who fought against the Soviets and before that tribal leaders who opposed the communist Afghan government. This sense of unending and ever morphing conflict is fatiguing.

Part II

Weaponized Narrative—Case Studies

Chapter 3

How China's Narrative Collapses Decision-Making and Creates Combined Effects

Brigadier General (retired) Thomas Drohan, Ph.D.

Narrative strategy is an integral part of China's combined effects warfare, which combines confrontation and cooperation. The process blends psychological-physical and preventive-causative effects. To better understand this approach, this chapter has three basic purposes. Namely, we will examine:

(1) how narrative strategy dupes victims into thoughtless orientation on their observations

(2) why a decision-making cycle should keep orientation and observation discrete yet combined

(3) how China wages narrative and combined effects warfare to envelop narrower strategies

We begin with a popular decision cycle: the OODA Loop. Observe, Orient, Decide, and Act (OODA) is a powerful model for making decisions in competitive environments. Strategic use of information can defeat it. Understanding narrative strategies can protect it.

The basic idea of an OODA Loop is to operate in a fast and relevant decision cycle while getting an opponent to make slow or irrelevant decisions. Information can defeat decision cycles by collapsing Observe and Orient (OO) into a single step. So that we *ingest* information. "Smart" 5G networks make us more susceptible to this, with the illusion that faster is smarter. The problem is that if we simply absorb more information, we think like a 1G computer:

- We accept only structured data (Observe only what Orient allows)
- We process data into information using one programmed language (Orient on limited meanings)
- We produce repetitive tasks (Decide and Act predictably)

As a result, we are reduced to less than machine learning. Even narrowly intelligent machines accept unstructured data, process data in multiple languages, and produce innovative solutions.[69]

How can we out-think unrestricted warriors in an environment filled with uncertain information and fast-processing machines?[70]

We can begin by understanding what strategic narratives are and what they do to our ability to make informed decisions. The OODA Loop is a demonstrative target because it is seductively simple in concept yet vulnerably complex in application. In this chapter, we use information tracked by the Hamilton 2.0 Dashboard of the Alliance for Securing Democracy and Dr. Ajit Maan's model of terrorist recruitment narrative in *Plato's Fear* to show the following:[71]

- How narrative strategy dupes victims into an Observe & Orient shortcut (O&O)
- Why Observe and Orient should be discrete but combined

OODA Meets Narrative Strategy

Colonel John Boyd's OODA Loop began as a fighter pilot's technique to shoot down enemy aircraft before they did the same to him.[72] OODA had to be fast, accurate, and holistic enough to anticipate changes in the environment:

---

[69] Max Tegmark, "Benefits and Risks of Artificial Intelligence," Future of Life Institute, accessed on October 26, 2020, https://futureoflife.org/background/benefits-risks-of-artificial-intelligence/?cn-reloaded=1&cn-reloaded=1; Justin Clegg, "The Impact of Machine Learning on Unstructured Data," *Medium*, uploaded on November 18. 2019, https://medium.com/@jclegg/the-impact-of-machine-learning-on-unstructured-data-23012e9e1428; David Intersimone, "Polyglot Programming—Development in Multiple Languages," *Computerworld*, uploaded on November 3, 2009, https://www.computerworld.com/article/2467812/polyglot-programming----development-in-multiple-languages.html; Bernard Marr, "27 Incredible Examples of AI and Machine Learning in Practice," *Forbes*, uploaded on April 30, 2018, https://www.forbes.com/sites/bernardmarr/2018/04/30/27-incredible-examples-of-ai-and-machine-learning-in-practice/#3ae6c68d7502.

[70] Qiao Liang and Wang Xiangsui, *Unrestricted Warfare* (Beijing: PLA Literature and Arts Publishing House, 1999).

[71] Hamilton 2.0 Dashboard, Alliance for Securing Democracy, accessed on October 26, 2020, https://securingdemocracy.gmfus.org/hamilton-dashboard/; Ajit Maan, *Plato's Fear* (Washington, DC: Narrative Strategies Ink, 2020).

[72] EricHall, "Col. John Boyd (1927–1997)," YouTube, uploaded on December 4, 2008, https://www.youtube.com/watch?v=ivTBv3wnp1Y&feature=emb_title.

Figure 1: OODA Loop

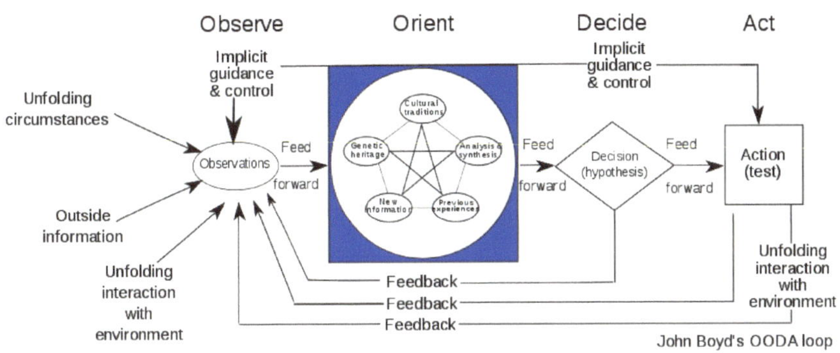

An in-depth explanation of the entire OODA Loop is beyond our scope here. A comprehensive collection of Boyd's briefings, and the articles and books about his thinking, can be found on Chet Richards' website.[73] However, many who have written about the OODA Loop regard the Orient phase as the most important one, myself included. This focus, nevertheless, gives short shrift to Observe, even as technology is expanding it.

Observe and Orient

Orientation is our mental perception of the world.[74] This cognitive process may happen in an instant, but it is a complex environmental outcome. Boyd described its determinants as interactions among heritage and culture, analysis and synthesis, historical experience and new information. Technological advancements enable us to observe more, from mechanical gauges that sense pressure to spectrometers that sense electromagnetic radiation. So much so that we have more observations on which to fixate. Or, on which to lose focus and become disoriented in a flood of data and information. We seek the best of both—details in context.

Fixation and lack of focus pose acute problems for our OODA, because we are supposed to orient on an observation to figure out what it means. If we fixate on data and orient it into a narrow context, the information is minimally useful. If we fail to orient data into a context

[73] Chet Richards' website, Slightly East of New, accessed on October 26, 2020, https://slightlyeastofnew.com.
[74] John R. Boyd, "Organic Design for Command and Control" (PowerPoint Presentation, Defense and the National Interest, Bluffton, South Carolina, September, 2014), slide 13.

at all, we get meaningless information. Our struggle in-between these extremes leads us toward a variety of frameworks, algorithms and networks. This is where narratives enter to play a strategic role, at a subliminal level.

Narrative as Strategy

Narrative strategy is "changing the way power works."[75] The Narrative Strategies (NS) team of scholars and professionals delves into the many ways and means of how to include narrative warfare in strategic influence, terrorism and insurgency, violent extremism, radicalization, information warfare, and social media studies. For our purpose of focusing on how narrative strategy can impede OODA, we will use the following definition of narrative: "Narrative is a method whereby the experiences of a life time can be provided with meaning by tying them together in a certain 'culturally sanctioned' structure."[76]

From this perspective, narratives are taken-for-granted cultural contexts that provide meaning. For instance, being "Chinese" means identifying with harmonious traditions from a long-standing China-centric civilization—without consciously thinking about it. Being "American" means identifying with democratic values of freedom and equality. While their details can be contentious (one might wonder who imposes harmony and what kind of freedom and equality, for instance), narratives are baked-in expectations of one's environment. As such, they are tacit sources of stories, stories that become narratives by expressing meaning. As a method, this has strategic implications for observation and orientation.

What we observe may be "true" empirically, but how we frame our observations is what assigns meaning, or significance, to them. Sometimes we are enculturated to accept deformed facts because they conform to our narratives. We disinform ourselves. Let's see how this can happen in an OODA Loop.

For Boyd, observing meant using human insight and vision to detect and monitor changing conditions (circumstances, interactions, and outside information in Figure 1 above).[77] If we can change more quickly than an adversary, we put ourselves in a position to

[75] Narrative Strategies team, "Law Enforcement Training—Deter Civil Strife," Narrative Strategies website, accessed on October 26, 2020, https://www.narrative-strategies.com.
[76] Ajit Maan, *Internarrative Identity: Placing the Self* (Lanham, MD: University Press of America, 2010), xvi.
[77] Boyd, "Organic Design for Command and Control," slides 3–4.

gain advantage. This sensing function is part of our implicit guidance and control (see Figure 1). This is like a command & control (C2) system, or an Operating System (OS) in a computer. Our basic C2 or OS instructs us to observe for a purpose. Generally it's to orchestrate actions for desired effects. Details matter.

For instance, if our C2 model is built around the need to process messages (technology can do that), how will we manage the command part of C2?[78] That requires leaders with a broader view of C2's purposes. If our C2 over-emphasizes proactive command, how will we manage individual biases? That requires leaders with mature situational awareness. An OS under the control of human or artificial intelligence is similarly constrained by learned or programmed intent. Predatory C2 and OS that exploit biases can undermine observation and orientation.

Ideology as Command & Control

Ideology is such a C2 system, one that orients its preys' observations to overpower its ideas. Make no mistake: both authoritarian and democratic societies are filled with ideologies and ideologues. The aims of ideological C2 systems tend to be exceptionalist, as in the following claims:

- The only just interpretation of Islam (Islamic State in the Levant)[79]
- The only legitimate Party to govern China (Communist Party)[80]
- The only leader who can reclaim Russian pride of place (Putinism)[81]
- The only political tradition that represents true American ideals (liberalism versus conservatism)[82]

All pure ideologies rob individuals of freedom to observe and orient on problems. Used strategically to achieve desired effects, they arrange information into purposed narratives.

---

[78] Carl H. Builder, Steven C. Bankes, and Richard Nordin, "Alternative Models of Command and Control," *Command Concepts: A Theory Derived from the Practice of Command and Control* (Santa Monica, CA: RAND Corporation, 1999), 127–36.

[79] "Isis Media," *VoxPol*, accessed on October 26, 2020, https://www.voxpol.eu/tag/isis-media/.

[80] See People's Daily coverage, *People's Daily*, accessed on October 26, 2020, http://en.people.cn.

[81] Konstantin Gaaze, "The True Nature of Putinism," *The Moscow Times*, posted on October 21, 2019, https://www.themoscowtimes.com/2019/10/21/the-true-nature-of-putinism-a67820.

[82] Chris Cillizza, "Donald Trump's Deeply Twisted Idea of American Exceptionalism," *CNN*, updated on January 6, 2020, https://www.cnn.com/2020/01/06/politics/donald-trump-iran-soleimani/index.html; Andrew O'Reilly, "Trump Sings Praises of American Exceptionalism in Elaborate July 4 Salute," *Fox News*, posted on July 4, 2019, https://www.foxnews.com/politics/trump-sings-praises-of-american-exceptionalism-in-elaborate-july-4-salute.

Strategic Use of Mis- Dis- Mal-Information

Ideologies and narrative strategies select, omit and manipulate information. Some information is true and some is false, often partly so. The use of true but harmful information, and false information—intentionally so or not, creates what Wardle and Derakhshan describe as information disorder.[83] This threat erodes trust on a global scale. The following definitions are from their Council of Europe report:[84]

- Mis-information: when false information is shared, but no harm is meant
- Dis-information: when false information is knowingly shared to cause harm
- Mal-information: when genuine information is shared to cause harm, often by moving information designed to stay private into the public sphere

What can we do?

A Solution

We can keep Observation and Orientation consciously discrete and consciously combined. Doing both is necessary because the two processes interact with each other. Separating O and O enables us to observe complex problems *and* be aware of how we orient to frame them. If we fail to do this, we are likely to be blind to unfamiliar problems and exclude relevant solutions. This filtering leads to sub-optimal decisions and actions. Combining separately conducted O and O prevents conflated O&O as a cause of decision loop collapse.

[83] Claire Wardle and Hossein Derakhshan, "Information Disorder: Toward an Interdisciplinary Framework for Research and Policy Making," Council of Europe, October, 2017.

[84] Wardle and Derakhshan, "Information Disorder."

Figure 2: Simplified OOAD Loop

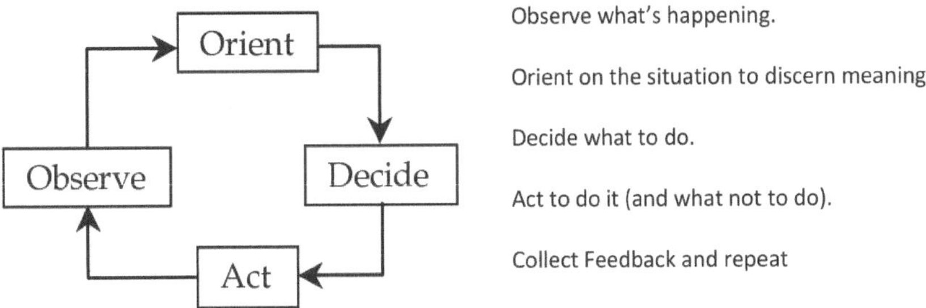

Having merged a decision cycle with narrative strategy, we are better armed to understand how strategic use of information can con observation and orientation into a single cursory step. Weaponized and delivered, information becomes a stratagem that denies its victims an independent capability to sense what is happening and to discern meaning.

How Information Crashes a Decision Cycle

Narratives are so powerful, Maan explains in *Plato's Fear*, because they evoke emotion that overrides reason.[85] Powerful narratives create receptive audiences by appealing to the internalized identities that organize their experiences, sub-consciously. The four-stage model explicated in this book in terms of identity and meaning describes how narratives are weaponized.

A Weaponized Narrative

The following figure captures important aspects of each stage in this psychological assault, as well as what is happening to an OODA decision-making process:

[85] Ajit Maan, *Plato's Fear* (Washington DC: Narrative Strategies Ink, 2020), 12–13.

Figure 3: Narrative Weaponization Model

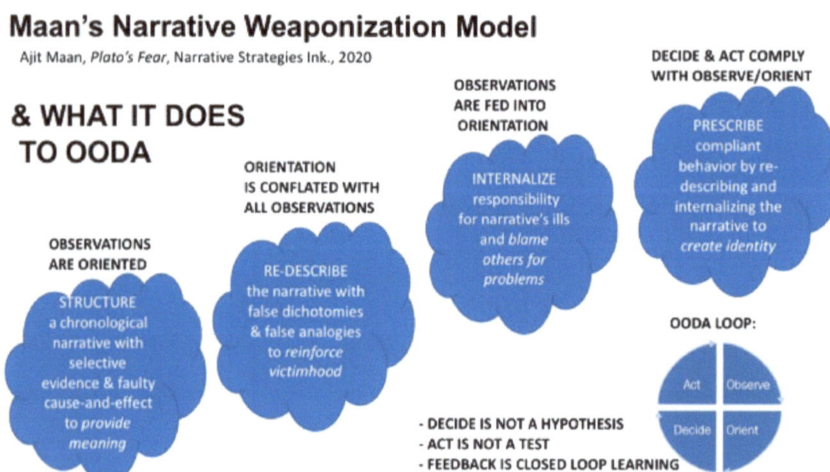

As an assembled weapon system, the last step in the process exploits all previous steps, creating a non-falsifiable belief system. Like a nationalism or religion, it has emotional appeal. That total impact on the OODA Loop is indicated on the bottom of the figure. Decisions and actions reinforce oriented observations.

The above cycle may seem abstract, so let's see some evidence. Using the italicized ideas above as pointers, we discover ample examples of Chinese information tracked by Hamilton 2.0. In a few places, I have inserted comments (marked by "Note:") to provide a comparison or explanation.

A Scattered Mass Campaign

Hamilton 2.0 is a visual analytics dashboard of narratives pushed by China and Russia government officials and state-funded media on Twitter, YouTube, sponsored websites, and at United Nations.[86] The tool provides a starting point for more in-depth analysis by scraping and processing data, then converting it into a tracker.

Ideally we would track official China's information all of the time, looking for structure, re-description, internalization and prescription. To establish a baseline inference for further study, on April 9-10, we looked at the top 10 Tweets (by Retweets and Likes) and posted Broadcasts over the preceding five-day period. This time segment was the middle of the COVID-19 pandemic for many parts of the globe.

A Disciplined Stream

- Structure
    - Chronological Sequence
        - CNN makes many mistakes in reporting
        - China will fight the pandemic for all mankind
        - China has never blocked medical purchases for Brazil
        - China mourns the fallen in this pandemic
        - China condemns US politician for rumoring about Chinese religious affairs and called on US to stop smearing China (Note: the same day the US Congress condemned China for its brutality against Muslims)
        - China hands over medical supplies to Afghanistan
        - Tehran conducts anti-COVID-19 operations
        - California 3D prints medical supplies due to shortages in US
        - New Delhi has adequate supplies amid coronavirus lockdown
        - China's new space-tracking ship is in the Atlantic
        - US Navy fires captain but crew applauds him
        - 87-year old Chinese COVID-19 patient plays violin for his caregivers
        - US expats in Mexico are stranded and choose to stay there
        - Wuhan bounces back from COVID-19
        - As pandemic spreads in US the bunker business is surging

---

86 Hamilton 2.0 Dashboard, Alliance for Securing Democracy, accessed on October 26, 2020, https://securingdemocracy.gmfus.org/hamilton-dashboard/

- Venezuelans need access to clean water
- Spain is #2 in COVID-19 cases, after the US
- Chinese embassies mourn pandemic victims
- Canada warns US against stopping medical shipments
- US stocks have worst quarter since 2008
- US company Johnson&Johnson plans to have vaccine by 2021
- Prominent US economist is on unemployment
- Johns Hopkins University Researchers create interactive COVID-19 map
- Brazilian doctor researches COVID-19 in lab
- Venezuela faces shortages of gasoline due to collapsed productivity and US sanctions
- China is cooperating with Brazil
- China resists racism and awaits apology from Brazil Minister of Education (note: Minister of Education Abraham Weintraub tweeted in a mock Chinese accent that China is using the pandemic for geopolitical advantage)
- UK thanked China for its help against the pandemic
- Chinese ambassador to Brazil spoke to the Minister of Health about strengthening cooperation
- China informed the US about the coronavirus back in January
- Chinese medical team arrives in Manila to help
- US vineyards brace for economic hit
- The idea that China is seeking geopolitical advantage while fighting the pandemic is ridiculous
- CDC recommends cloth masks as 1000 deaths mark another sad day in the US
- US trade embargo blocks critical aid to Cuba
- Multinational corporations meet in China to discuss resuming production
- Chinese students are leaving the US because schools are closed

        - Chinese retailers and celebrities are live-streaming products to bring business back
        - Bodies in the streets of Ecuador
        - Wuhan lifts its lockdown
        - Brazil has a surplus in trade with China and deficit in trade with the US
        - China is cooperating with Italy in a quid pro quo against the pandemic

    - Faulty cause and effect & selective evidence
        - US reporting is biased, which creates fake news about China (Note: based on one example that I could not find; there are many examples of CNN stories on that date about China's lack of transparency regarding COVID-19)
        - China fights the pandemic in cooperation with others for the good of mankind, not for geopolitical advantage (Note: Weintraub—"When the crisis erupted, instead of alerting the world, they withheld information and rushed to build respirators, which they're now selling to a world that's desperate for them")
        - Brazil's trade surplus with China contrasts with how US treats Brazil (Note: China's overall trade balance with the world is a $368b surplus)
        - US sanctions hurt Venezuela, Cuba and Iran as they struggle against the pandemic

- Redescription
    - Artificial dichotomies & false analogies
        - US does false reporting while China is transparent
        - US runs trade surpluses with other countries while China runs deficits
        - Brazil has a Minister of Education who is racist while China resists racism
        - China repaid Italy's kindness by donating medical supplies, sending medical experts to Italy, and facilitating Italy's purchase of medical

supplies from China (Note: several US media outlets report that China is selling Italy medical supplies that Italy had donated to China)

- US stock market is in decline while large corporations will soon resume production in China
- The apparently positive Johnson&Johnson and Johns Hopkins University topics create negative comparisons—a US vaccine is a year away and JHU's map shows US COVID cases rising/China recovering
- The US is warned by Canada to not cut off medical supplies while China supplies Afghanistan, the Philippines, the UK and Brazil
- Wuhan is bouncing back from the pandemic while US deaths are still rising
- The US Navy fires a captain of an aircraft carrier while a new Chinese ship tracks satellites from the Atlantic

- Internalization
  - Take responsibility to blame others
    - Brazil is racist not China
    - The US hurts Brazil's balance of trade while China helps
    - The US hurts Cuba and Venezuela with sanctions during this epidemic
    - China is not to blame for the pandemic
    - We must all work together in this "Battle of Moscow" against the virus
    - US politicians spread false rumors about religion in China
    - China informed the US about the virus in January

- Prescription
  - Identify and comply with narrative
    - Note: so far the Brazilian government has not taken any action to correct or apologize to China for Minister of Education Weintraub's remarks (he is under fire for non-China related remarks, too)
    - President Bolsonaro's son, Eduardo regularly Tweets against the "Chinese virus" and the Chinese "dictatorship"; reports that "Brazil has joined ranks

with US politicians in insinuating that China was behind the coronavirus outbreak"

- Further aspects of this spat may be found at #TradeBlockadeOnChinaNow, trending in Brazil

Narrative Analysis

China's official information flow fits the Maan model in all respects. We examine how for each of the four elements of the narrative. From the content above, we derive China's basic narrative as:

China is a benign and blameless model of global cooperation

Structure

The narrative's structure consists of disciplined faulty cause-and-effect logic and selective use of evidence.

Discipline comes in as leader's intent and Party doctrine. This is standard operating procedure for the Communist Party of China, especially since the elevation of Xi Jinping, who is General Secretary of the Communist Party, Chairman of the Central Military Commission, and Preeminent (or Core) Leader.[87] Moreover, his thought has doctrinal status.[88]

The causes are faulty in an under-determined way, which may not be obvious to uninformed or indoctrinated observers.[89] Under-determined arguments cite causes (such as US sanctions) of effects (such as Venezuela's economic and COVID-related struggles) as if they are the only causes of the effects. It's up to the reader/listener to think of alternative explanations. Other determining factors (such as corruption in Venezuela) are not mentioned.

Many effects related to COVID-19 are omitted—such as Chinese authorities delaying notification about the outbreak and under-reporting COVID cases. So are their causes—such

[87] Nikhil Sonnad, "Xi Jinping is not the 'President' of China," *Quartz*, posted on November 2, 2017, https://qz.com/1112638/xi-jinping-title-xi-jinping-is-not-the-president-of-china.

[88] Michael Martina and Philip Wen, "China's Communist Party Elevates Xi Doctrine, Cementing His Power," *Huffpost*, accessed on October 26, 2020, https://www.huffpost.com/entry/chinas-communist-party-elevates-xi-doctrine-cementing-his-power_n_59ef2d18e4b07cf8380c528c.

[89] *Your Dictionary*, "Underdetermine," accessed on October 26, 2020. The term is defined as "to provide too few constraints to specify a unique solution."

as systematic suppression of dissent in China. Unless the reader has a broad orientation or is broadly familiar with the topic, these tricks escape observation. The risks of running a free press in China further empower the Party-government narrative.

Social media assists selective use of evidence. To wit, 280-character-or-less Tweets. With such small space for puny attention spans (on the order of 40-100 characters max), short posts are defensibly effective.[90] This works en masse and over time. ReTweets are particularly guilty of disseminating like-filtered thinking because they overwhelmingly are sent by those who agree with the original message.

Overall, the narrative's structure hides a globally obvious cause—China as the secretive initiator and negligent accelerator of the COVID-19 pandemic.

Re-description

Building upon the above structure, the narrative gets re-described via false analogies and opportunistic blaming of others. Re-telling the story with new metaphors and new partial content in different contexts helps calcify the threat of new ideas, in two ways. First, loyal repetition buries inconvenient facts (COVID-19 emanated from China). Second, nuanced repetition raises new facts (US surpasses China in COVID-19 deaths). Done repeatedly, repeatedly, audiences lose the particulars of contexts (China-US differences with respect to sharing public health information and accurately reporting deaths). The new context becomes the repeated narrative itself.

Overall, re-description of the narrative spews thoroughly negative coverage of the US paired with thoroughly positive coverage of China. This dichotomy invents differences. If sustained and thoughtlessly absorbed as received truth, the stratagem preempts questioning the narrative.

Internalization

There is plenty of urging others to blame others. Such stoking is easy to do during a global crisis. Even if internalization does not recruit many sympathizers, blaming others helps

---

[90] Kevan Lee, "The Proven Ideal Length of Every Tweet, Facebook Post, and Headline Online," *Fast Company*, posted on July 4, 2014, https://www.fastcompany.com/3028656/the-proven-ideal-length-of-every-tweet-facebook-post-and-headline-online.

authorities deflect attention away from domestic grievances. It seems doubtful that blaming rivals during a pandemic which originated in China will attract more adherents. Similarly, we do not expect the narrative will perpetuate itself outside China.

The main reason is the circularity of the narrative—China is benign and blameless because China does benign and blameless things. Cyclical thinking is certainly appealing. However, this narrative is testable. It follows that those with access to evidence that contradicts the narrative are not likely to embrace it unless doing so serves their interests.

Prescription

If people identify with a narrative, they conform to what it says. This implies accepting official China's version of benign behavior. With regard to the People's Republic, that means going along with Beijing's blameless aggression in Tiananmen Square, Xinjiang, Tibet, Hong Kong, Taiwan, South China Sea, East China Sea, Vietnam, Myanmar, Aksai Chin, Kashmir, and the Ussuri River. Completing the narrative's circular reasoning, China's interests are global interests. Is this far-fetched?

Caution: beware in a world victimized by global threats.

China's narrative is utopian (benign and blameless authoritarian governance), with a conflicted middle (arguably where we are now), and a conclusion to act for a better future (more order, less chaos). China's proposed new order is cloaked by claims of cooperation. The myth contains all of the elements of a strategic narrative.

Combined Effects Warfare

So far, we have completed two of our three purposes: showing how narrative strategy dupes victims into taking an Observe & Orient shortcut; and explaining why Observe and Orient should be discrete yet holistically combined. Narratives influence decision makers psychologically to produce a variety of effects, some anticipated and some not.

Our third purpose is to reveal how China wages combined effects warfare to envelop narrower strategies. To do this, we use a language of cooperation and confrontation drawn from combined effects strategy.[91]

As depicted in Figure 4 below, the framework encompasses psychological means and physical means to prevent action and to cause action. These actions are the strategy's effects, ranging from "Dissuade" in the upper left to "Coerce" in the bottom right. The two basic distinctions of cooperative and confrontational interactions generate four spectra of effects with opposite endpoints:

Cooperative:

Dissuade (Ds) ——————— Persuade (P)
Secure (S) ————————— Induce (I)

Confrontational:

Deter (Dt) —————————Compel (Cp)
Defend (Df) ———————— Coerce (Cr)

In the real world, we see blends of each type of effect. China typically leads with some sort of Inducement. To describe such sorts, we categorize them generally as Diplomatic, Informational, Military, Economic, and Social (DIMES). US national security, defense, and military strategies routinely ignore Social-cultural.

We can use these simple distinctions to characterize effects in a complex information environment. Some of the effects can be attributed to causes, some not so much, and all feature uncertainty. All effects become potential causes of other effects.

Orienting on observations this way can inform decisions and actions about how to anticipate and create effects. In the competitive world, psychological and physical means can create synergistic, superior combinations of effects.

[91] Thomas A. Drohan, *A New Strategy for Complex Warfare: Combined Effects in East Asia* (Amherst, NY: Cambria Press, 2016).

Figure 4: Combined Effects Strategy

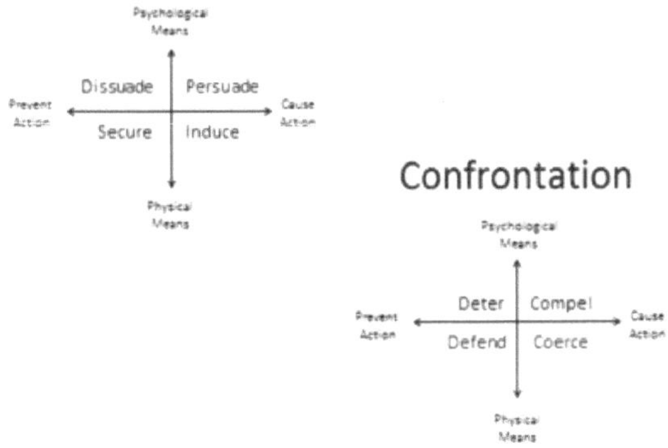

How Narrative Creates Psychological Effects

Using this combined effects language, China's narrative (as inferred from our sample) works by Inducing its targets to reach favored conclusions. This is done through a "collapse and influence" mechanism:

1. Collapse a target's Orientation on the environment. As previously described, the narrative gets the victim to conflate Orientation and Observation. Over time, the targeted victim may accept China's narrative. Meanwhile, the narrative also works to do the following.
2. Influence the target's will and capability to Observe. This reorientation affects how the target Decides and Acts. To understand this, we turn to a logic of targeting will and capability.

The following line-of-effect logic can apply to any audience. Referring to Figure 4's various types of effects, the narrative is a psychological method that produces four types of psychological effects. Following each effect's logic is an example from official China's information campaign... followed by one example of an effect (attributed intent):

Line-of-effect Logic:

a. Assure an audience's Will... to Persuade

Example: China assures the will of Italians by donating medical supplies, sending medical experts, and facilitating purchases... to persuade NATO members that Italy's donated medical supplies to China were not subsequently sold to Italy, but instead constituted a mutually beneficial quid pro quo.

b. Intimidate an audience's Will... to Compel

Example: China intimidates the will of Brazilians to tolerate Minister of Education Weintraub's anti-China remarks by referring to Brazil's trade surplus with China... to compel an apology that acknowledges respect of China (Weintraub subsequently promised to apologize if China furnished 1000 ventilators to hospitals in Brazil).[92]

c. Enhance an audience's Capability... to dissuade

Example: China enhances the capability of countries (Afghanistan, Brazil, Cuba, Iran, the Philippines, UK) fighting the pandemic for the good of mankind... to dissuade the notion that China provides aid to gain geopolitical advantage.

d. Neutralize an audience's Capability... to deter

---

[92] Eduardo Simões, "Brazil-China Diplomatic Spat Escalates Over Coronavirus Supplies," *Reuters*, updated on April 6, 2020, https://www.reuters.com/article/us-health-coronavirus-brazil/brazil-china-diplomatic-spat-escalates-over-coronavirus-supplies-idUSKBN21O22Z.

Example: China threatens to neutralize US access to medical supplies from China in retaliation for the US travel ban on China... to deter further US actions with negative economic impact on China.[93]

How well an activity works in achieving these psychological effects depends on the audience. An activity intended to assure or intimidate someone's will, or enhance or neutralize their capability, will be filtered not only by the orientation of the targeted audience, but also non-targeted actors. Instant communication globalizes the observation of local activities to many actors. This creates huge space for misunderstanding and distorting psychological effects in local contexts, without being there.

Cultural analysis is critical to understanding how actors contextualize data and process information. The cultural elements of orientation include identity and the "cognitive frameworks with which we organize the influx of information to our brains."[94] To anticipate how audiences frame the meaning of an activity, baseline intelligence products must address narrative and internarrative analyses.

In a pervasive information environment that can empower any activity, narrative warfare has become a struggle for command and control of psychological and physical effects.

Physical & Psychological Effects and Narrative Warfare

In addition to multi-layered and variable psychological effects, we need to understand the added value of physical effects. China's history is replete with combining physical with psychological *effects* through strategies of confrontation *and* cooperation. Perhaps the clearest set of examples are territorial disputes.

Since the establishment of the People's Republic in 1949, China has used combined effects strategy against every one of its contiguous neighbors to re-expand ("liberate") imperial borders. Here are three illustrative examples of combined effects that involve several types of physical and psychological effects.

---

[93] "Confidently, the World Should Thank China," *Xinhuanet*, updated on March 4, 2020, http://www.xinhuanet.com/2020-03/04/c_1125660473.htm. My translation.

[94] Ajit Maan, *Plato's Fear*, 29.

1. Tibet: Coerce and Compel, followed by Induce, Coerce and Persuade (Cr Cp I P)

China coerced an occupation of Tibet in 1950, then compelled its absorption into the People's Republic as the Tibet Autonomous Region in 1965. In 1995, Beijing induced ethically Han Chinese businesses into Tibet, and continues to socially coerce and persuade Tibetans to accept "Chinese" culture and law. This overall synergy of effects increases the impact of China's occupation and absorption of Tibet.

Today, the basic strategy is to persuade, induce, compel and coerce nationalism to strengthen Beijing's central authority.

Narrative Warfare in Tibet is a battle over identity. Beijing seeks to erase Tibetan identity as separate from Han "Chinese" identity. What Tsering Topgyal refers to as "identity insecurity" and loyalty to the Dalai Lama explains Tibetans' persistent resistance.[95] Beijing's physical and psychological assault to out-populate and crush the will of free Tibet continues.

2. Taiwan: Compel and Induce (Cp I)

China continues to compel polarized politics in Taiwan to create a domestic dilemma with respect to unification with and independence from mainland China. China then induces that dilemma with economic incentives and military maneuvers. This combination targets the society and in particular the independence-leaning Democratic Progressive Party and the unification-leaning Kuomintang Party.

Today, the basic strategy is to compel and induce Taiwan's dependence on China while dividing Taiwan's politics.

Narrative warfare in Taiwan is reflected on two battlefronts. First, China and Taiwan compete for international recognition and supply chain control: dependence versus diversification. Second, China pursues cultural dominance by emphasizing a common "Chinese" (read Han) identity. As Taiwan's demographics overwhelm "pure" Chinese, Taiwan's population is becoming distinctively Taiwanese.[96]

---

[95] Tsering Topgyal, "Identity Insecurity and the Tibetan Resistance against China," *Pacific Affairs* 86, no. 3 (September 2013): 515–38.

[96] Keoni Everington, "Record 83% of People in Taiwan Identify as Taiwanese amid Wuhan Virus Outbreak," *Taiwan News*, posted on February 24, 2020, https://www.taiwannews.com.tw/en/news/3880591.

3. India and Pakistan: Secure, Coerce, Compel and Induce (S Cr Cp I)

China secures British non-intervention, seizes Aksai Chin from India (1962), then induces Pakistan to cede part of India-claimed Kashmir to China (1963). China's victory over India in 1962 not only coerced India's territorial loss, but also compelled closer China-Pakistan relations. The latter induced the territorial transfer.

Today, the basic strategy is to secure agreements that induce acceptance of China's terms, and compel and coerce compliance.

Narrative warfare among China, India and Pakistan is complex.

4. Japan and US: Induce, Dissuade, Persuade, Compel (I Ds P Cp)

China induces economic ties with Japan and the US, dissuades Japanese businesses from supporting Tokyo's claims to the Diaoyu Islets, persuades US elites of Beijing's legitimate counter-claims (ongoing Senkaku/Diaoyu dispute), and compels a Japan overreaction with US restraint.

Today, the basic strategy is to induce economic dependence, dissuade Japan from imperial-era territorial claims while persuading US agreement, and compel the separation of Japan from US military support. When China achieves local military superiority, the latter will escalate to coercion.

Narrative warfare involving China, Japan and the US involves the following: China's authoritarian condemnation of Japan's imperial past while extolling its own as Confucian benevolence; Japan's democratic ambivalent uniquism torn between its anti-militarist Peace Constitution (see Article 9) and behaving as a "normal country";[97] and US democratic exceptionalism.[98]

[97] Prime Minister of Japan and His Cabinet, "The Constitution of Japan," promulgated on November 3, 1946, accessed on October 26, 2020, https://japan.kantei.go.jp/constitution_and_government_of_japan/constitution_e.html, article 9; "Event Report: Japan as a Normal Country? Retrospect and Prospect," *The Journal of Contemporary Asian Studies*, accessed on October 26, 2020, https://utsynergyjournal.org/2019/04/15/event-report-japan-as-a-normal-country-retrospect-and-prospect.

[98] Walter A. McDougall, "American Exceptionalism... Exposed," *Foreign Policy Research Institute E-Notes*, October, 2012, https://www.files.ethz.ch/isn/161931/201210.mcdougall.americanexceptionalism.pdf.

Concluding Thoughts

Strategic use of information delivered in a meaningful narrative can collapse a decision loop, converting a speedy decision cycle into a vulnerability. A basic desired effect of this weaponized information assault is to Induce conclusions, which can be combined with many other psychological and physical effects.

China's waging of combined effects warfare around its periphery to re-expand its borders is an empirical fact obscured by the assumption that war has to be violent. In reality, the destruction of critical thought is a most profound combined effect and can precede, accompany, and replace kinetic warfare. Once observation and orientation are conflated, thinking flows in a closed circuit. To avoid this, we need to keep the O's separate, but combined in a holistic decision-making process.

Why separate? Observation should not be influenced too much by orientation, if we are to see what is really happening. Orientation is for assigning meaning to observations after the observations have been made. This can happen in nanoseconds via human intuition and "fast" thinking, or AI.[99] For the former, we need to be aware of our own biases (experience-based and cognitive).[100] For the latter, we need to know the bias (bias-variance relationship) in that neural network.[101]

Whether the orientation is being done by humans, machines, or the interface of both, orientation must be functionally separate or deep enough (multi-layered learning) to avoid replicating observation.[102] Fused O&O does not learn; it is predictably repetitive.

Why combined? When we combine the effects of O and O, we can get more competitive results.

Observation's effects include interactive relationships in the information environment, not just objects in that environment.

---

[99] Daniel Kahneman, *Thinking Fast and Slow* (New York: Farrar, Straus and Giroux, 2011).

[100] Jens Pohl, "Intuition: Role, Biases, Cognitive Basis, and a Hypothetical Synergistic Explanation of Intuitive Brain Operations, InterSymp-2017, July 31, 2017, https://digitalcommons.calpoly.edu/cgi/viewcontent.cgi?article=1107&context=cadrc; Christopher Dwyer, "12 Common Biases that Affect How We Make Everyday Decisions," *Psychology Today*, posted on September 7, 2018, https://www.psychologytoday.com/us/blog/thoughts-thinking/201809/12-common-biases-affect-how-we-make-everyday-decisions.

[101] MissingLink, "Neural Network Bias: Bias Neuron, Overfitting and Underfitting," *MissingLink*, accessed on October 26, 2020, https://missinglink.ai/guides/neural-network-concepts/neural-network-bias-bias-neuron-overfitting-underfitting.

[102] Guru99, "Deep Learning Tutorial for Beginners: Neural Network Classification" *Guru99*, accessed on October 26, 2020, https://www.guru99.com/deep-learning-tutorial.html.

For instance, we saw that China's narrative includes these observations: US COVID-19 deaths are on the rise while China's are in decline; and, China sent a medical team to the Philippines to fight COVID-19 while the US threatens to reduce medical supplies to an ally.

These observations interact with each other to fashion a desired conclusion: China can and will help us more than the US can and will. Rather than jump to such pre-shaped conclusions, we need to treat each observation discretely. Then we can anticipate how all observations relate to and interact among various audiences. This gets into orientation.

Orientation's effects include the conclusions of analysis and experience (see Figure 1). This is our best defense against an ideological narrative that seeks to induce our conclusions. We also need to create causative effects. Critical thinking in the form of advanced analysis (especially Information Environment Characterization), for instance, considers new information, culture, heritage, and observed interactions among linkages.[103] Applying this orientation to the observations in the previous paragraph discovers other factors that account for COVID-19 death rates and medical assistance:

- Death rates—data comprehensiveness, integrity of analysis, and dissemination of results[104]
- Medical assistance—timing of COVID-19 recovery (China first), China-Philippines territorial disputes, US COVID-19 aid to the Philippines, China-US-Philippines relations, and the US Defense Production Act impact on Canada[105]

---

[103] Larry Bruns et al., "Information Environment Advanced Analysis Course," JMark Services Inc., accessed on October 26, 2020, https://www.jmarkservices.com/information-environment-advanced-analysis-course, section on "Information Environment Characterization."

[104] Sion Davoudi, Julie A. Dooling, Barbara Glondys, Theresa D. Jones, Lesley Kadlec, Shauna M. Overgaard, Kerry Ruben, Annemarie Wendicke. "Data Quality Management Model (2015 Update)—Retired," *Journal of AHIMA* 86, no.10 (October 2015): expanded web version, section entitled Overview of the Data Quality Model.

[105] Lusha Zhang and Ryan Woo, "China Reports No New Coronavirus Deaths as Cases Decline," *U.S. News*, posted on April 6, 2020, https://www.usnews.com/news/world/articles/2020-04-06/mainland-china-reports-32-new-confirmed-cases-of-coronavirus; Amalie Henden, "South China Sea Dispute: China and Philippines Frictions Explained—What is Going On?" *Express*, published on June 30, 2019, https://www.express.co.uk/news/world/1147240/south-china-sea-dispute-explained-china-news-Philippines; Gaea Katreena Cabico, "US Pledges P139 Million Aid to Philippines for COVID-19 Response," *Philstar Global*, published on March 17, 2020, https://www.philstar.com/headlines/2020/03/17/2001608/us-pledges-p139-million-aid-philippines-covid-19-response; John J. Xenakis, "World View: Philippines President Duterte Says He Would Go to War Over South China Sea," *Breitbart*, published on May 30, 2018, https://www.breitbart.com/national-security/2018/05/30/30-may-18-world-view-philippine-president-duterte-reverses-position-says-he-would-go-to-war-with-china-over-south-china-sea/; Oliver Holmes, "Trump Hails 'Great Relationship' with Philippines' Duterte," *The Guardian*, published on November 13, 2017, https://www.theguardian.com/us-news/2017/nov/13/trump-hails-great-relationship-with-philippines-duterte; Ben Blanchard, "Duterte Aligns Philippines with China, says U.S. has Lost," *Reuters*, published on October 20, 2016, https://www.reuters.com/article/us-china-philippines-

Orientation, like observation, is a contest. A broad orientation on the information environment can anticipate China's activities, such as opportune assistance to states in territorial disputes with China and in security relationships with the US. With proactive analysis and a combined effects approach, China's inducement-dependent effects can be countered and subsumed. This requires a DIMES-wide strategy that sets and adjusts long-term conditions.

To induce us into desired conclusions, China' weaponized narrative spews forth in a scattered campaign with a relatively disciplined stream of information. It follows that we need to track official China's information flow over a longer period of time to evaluate its consistency.

Don't expect the regurgitated narrative to change until China's one-Party authoritarian system changes.

For now, we observe a narrative that orients its victims on a Party line fiction. Combined with other psychological effects and a full array of physical effects, that narrative can have disproportionate impact on vulnerable audiences. The contest over narrative strategy and conceptions of warfare requires serious attention and commitment. Out-thought is out-fought.

The art of war is of vital importance to the State. It is a matter of life and death, a road either to safety or to ruin. Hence it is a subject of inquiry which can on no account be neglected.[106]

– Sunzi, *The Art of War*

idUSKCN12K0AS; Richard Hall, "Trudeau Threatens Retaliation after Trump Keeps Shipment of Masks Intended for Canadian Doctors," *Independent*, published on April 3, 2020, https://www.independent.co.uk/news/world/americas/coronavirus-trump-trudeau-us-canada-face-masks-supplies-doctors-a9446841.html.

[106] Sun Tzu, *The Art of War*, translated by Lionel Giles, The Internet Classics Archive, accessed on October 26, 2020, http://classics.mit.edu/Tzu/artwar.html.

Chapter 4

How Russia's Narratives Reorient Decision-Making and Create Combined Effects

Brigadier General (retired) Thomas Drohan, Ph.D.

As a fellow traveler with China's strategy, Russia's use of narrative reorients decisions in an Observe-Orient-Decide-Act (OODA) Loop. The distortion of information is not just divisive. In a strategy of combined effects, narratives lead the synergy of psychological and physical warfare. The broad approach envelops narrower conceptions of warfare oblivious to information effects.

Official Russia's purpose in weaponizing information is to divide audiences, and in multiple ways. The divisiveness works by simultaneously persuading, compelling, dissuading and deterring behavior. As we will demonstrate, this approach envelops a narrower US conception of "when deterrence fails" warfare. Russia's narrative creates its combined effect by reorienting a target audience's understanding of what it observes. The new orientation attributes negative intent, sowing discontent and confusion about observations real and contrived.

Narrative as Initiative

Narratives wield profoundly powerful effects in the information environment. Consider initiative, a principle widely regarded as critical in offensive warfare. Psychological narratives create types of initiative that are difficult to defeat with physical force. Once digitized and disseminated via social media, narratives become information readily integrated into platforms and applications on a massive scale.

The power of narrative is illustrated by the following forms of initiative: tempo; momentum; learning; decision; position; and freedom of maneuver.[107] The second type in each pair below illustrates how narratives proliferate into influential places:

[107] Thomas A. Drohan, "Paper #20. Competing with Analog Weapons in a Digital Arena? How to Gain Advantage," International Center for Security and Leadership, published on February 27, 2020, https://securityandleadership.com/paper-20-gaining-advantage-an-analog-digital-comparative-approach.

Figure 1: Types of Initiative

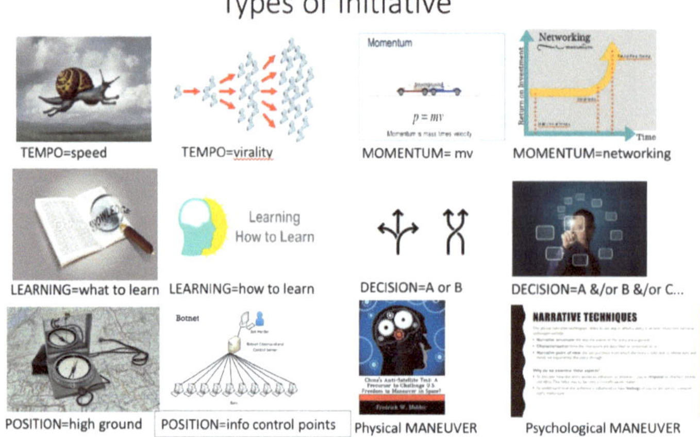

Narratives' success in achieving initiative does not mean greater lethality does not matter. It does mean that the information effects of lethality matter. When information is being contested and lethal capabilities are not, information can be divisively effective. How? By targeting will and capability.

The means of an influential narrative are both cooperative and confrontational, not just one or the other. This duality is effective across diverse contexts. Globally and locally, there are ample opportunities to assure will as well as to intimidate will; and to enhance capability as well as to neutralize capability. This flexibility to divide target audiences with opposing ideas can create relative weakness. From the perspective of the current Russian Federation regime, that is supposed to enhance national status and respect.

We use Colonel John Boyd's OODA Loop because it is an accepted decision-making process in both public and private sectors. Its strength is in making fast decisions in contested environments. Its weakness is susceptibility to mis-, dis-, and mal-information, which distorts perceptions.[108]

[108] Claire Wardle and Hossein Derakhshan, "Information Disorder: Toward an Interdisciplinary Framework for Research and Policy Making," Council of Europe, October, 2017.

Narrative warfare strategically arranges information. In manipulative blends of cooperation and confrontation, Russia's narratives work psychologically. In concert with physical strategies, the narratives also set conditions for synergistic effects.

Arranging Information

Russia's narrative warfare tries to detonate more effects on rivals than rivals can do to Russia. In contrast to China's single-Party narrative, Russia's is fragmented and does not offer a better future. So instead of fantasizing a Putin version of Xi's carefully arranged Chinese Dream, Russian narratives spout information to cultivate confusion. Why?

Internally, Moscow does not have the control over its population that Beijing manages to exert. To split authoritarian hairs, Russia is more of a pseudo-democracy than China.[109] Corruption complicates the flow of information. Putin's targeting of individuals to influence via organized crime compares to Xi's "anti-corruption" probes that purge rivals and use syndicates in state-owned enterprises.[110] With less state filtering of information and mass surveillance than in China, Russians can voice more discontent. In response, Russia's "digital authoritarianism" has become flexible to control a connected and engaged civil society.[111] After anti-government protests in 2011, state-run information outlets joined the stream of non-attributed cyber-attacks and troll & bot pollution.

Externally, pro-Russia criminals exploit grievances of marginalized Russian speakers in former Soviet republics. Russophones residing in free states after the USSR's demise are more vulnerable than China's diaspora that fled the PRC's rise. The Putin regime views territory from the Baltics to Georgia as breakaway states. From one extreme Eurasianist perspective, the rest of the Caucasus and Central Asian front is Russian space.[112] That message loses purchase in the 80% of Russian territory east of the Urals, where only 25% of Russia's

---

[109] Jamie Doward, "Putin Takes the Next Step to Staying in Power till 2036," *The Guardian*, posted on March 15, 2020, https://www.theguardian.com/world/2020/mar/15/power-bid-could-leave-vladimir-putin-in-charge-till-2036.

[110] Emily Couch, "Mark Galeotti: 'The Vory: Russia's Super Mafia'," *The Moscow Times*, published on May 5, 2019, https://www.themoscowtimes.com/2019/05/05/mark-galleotti-the-vory-russias-super-mafia-a65488; Sonny Shiu-Hing Lo, *The Politics of Controlling Organized Crime in Greater China* (London: Routledge, 2016).

[111] Alina Polyakova and Chris Meserole, "Exporting Digital Authoritarianism: The Russian and Chinese Models," Brookings Institution, August, 2019, https://www.brookings.edu/wp-content/uploads/2019/08/FP_20190827_digital_authoritarianism_polyakova_meserole.pdf.

[112] John B. Dunlop, "Aleksandr Dugin's Foundations of Geopolitics," *Demokratizatsiya* 12, no. 1 (January 2004): 41.

population lives.[113] At the same time, China is displacing Russian influence with continentally integrative networks of energy, trade, infrastructure, and finance.[114] Nordic states are resistant to Russian influence domestically but subject to Russian military activity in the Barents Sea.

That leaves Russian enclaves along Russia's western front to Ukraine as the most receptive to pro-Russia narratives. Estonia, Latvia, Lithuania, Moldova, Byelorus and Ukraine have Russian-speaking minorities whose multiple identities can be exploited. Moscow's divisive drive to regain control is a response to newly independent states joining NATO to be free of authoritarian domination. With Russians in Russia actively participating in domestic politics, the regime stirs up patriotism to deflect democratic reform and incite unrest abroad.

Russia's production of distracting information is extensive. Kompromat, active measures, and external political interference combine with direct and proxy aggression, as in Georgia (2008) and Ukraine (2014).[115] The COVID-19 pandemic is only the latest opportunity for Russia to deploy disinformation for strategic purposes.[116]

To understand how arranging information can impact and reorient decision-making, we look at narrative warfare in an OODA Loop.

Sense-Making

Both OODA and narrative strategy seek to create advantage in an environment by making sense of what is going on and proactively shaping "the fight."

Detailed in this book's China case,[117] the purpose of John Boyd's OODA Loop is to anticipate and shape changes in the environment:[118]

---

113 Alexander Kruglov, "The Chinese Influx into Asian Russia," *Asia Times*, published on June 13, 2019, https://asiatimes.com/2019/06/the-chinese-influx-into-asian-russia.

114 Kent E. Calder, *Super Continent: The Logic of Eurasian Integration* (Stanford, CA: Stanford University Press, 2019), 70–99.

115 Laura King and Ann M. Simmons, "Who, Us? Kremlin Says it Doesn't Engage in 'Kompromat', but History Suggests Otherwise," *Los Angeles Times*, published on January 11, 2017, https://www.latimes.com/world/europe/la-fg-russia-kompromat-20170111-story.html; Thomas Rid, *Active Measures: The Secret History of Disinformation and Political Warfare* (New York: Farrar, Straus, and Giroux, 2020).

116 Robin Emmott, "Russia Deploying Coronavirus Disinformation to Sow Panic in West, EU Document Says," *Reuters*, published on March 18, 2020, https://www.reuters.com/article/us-health-coronavirus-disinformation/russia-deploying-coronavirus-disinformation-to-sow-panic-in-west-eu-document-says-idUSKBN21518F.

117 See chapter 3.

118 ErieHall, "Col. John Boyd (1927–1997)," YouTube, uploaded on December 4, 2008, https://www.youtube.com/watch?v=ivTBv3wnp1Y&feature=emb_title.

Figure 2: OODA Loop

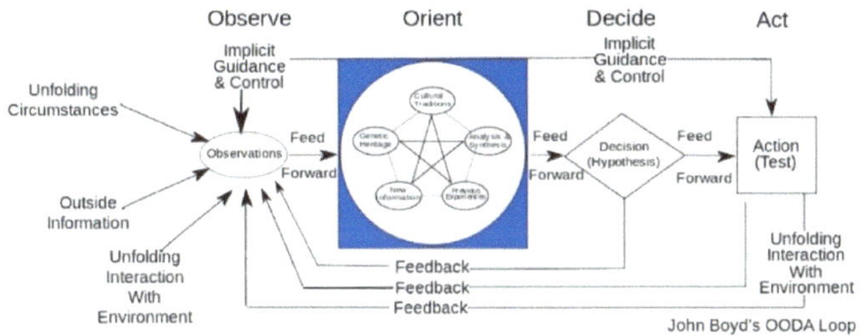

The Observe and Orient phases are key because they condition the Decide and Act phases—what to do and what not to do. Fixating on what's observed or not having a focus at all distorts orientation, which is our mental perception of what's going on. Many factors go into orientation to figure out what the observations mean to us. This creation of a context is where a narrative enters to shape meaning.

That in turn influences decisions and behavior.

Weaponizing a Narrative

As detailed in the China case,[119] Dr. Maan's narrative weaponization model in *Plato's Fear* explains how extremist narratives develop:[120]

---

[119] See chapter 3 of this book.
[120] Ajit Maan, *Plato's Fear* (Washington, DC: Narrative Strategies Ink, 2020).

Figure 3: Narrative Weaponization Model

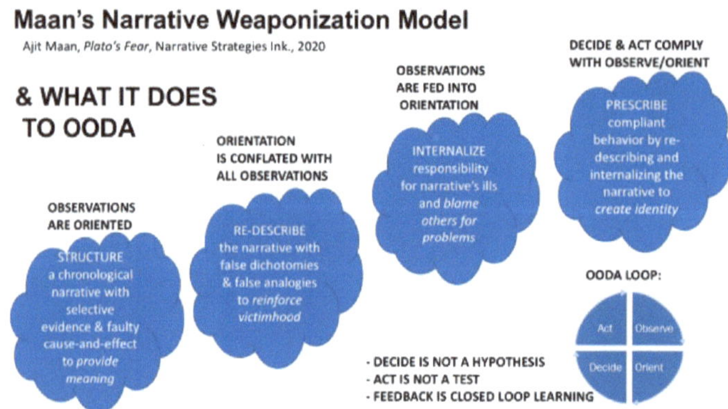

The following describes *the gist* of each step in Figure 2, and what is happening to OODA:

- Structure: *selective evidence* and *faulty cause-and-effect* chronologies trick vulnerable victims into Orienting on Observations in a desired way
- Re-description: *artificial dichotomies* and *false analogies* proliferate the narrative to further conflate Orientation with Observations
- Internalization: as re-described Observations reinforce the Orientation, victims assume internal responsibility to *externalize blame*
- Prescription: identifying with the *narrative prescribes* circular behavior: Observe & Orient fit the narrative; Decide & Act are compliant

A useful way to categorize the selective evidence, faulty cause-and-effect, artificial dichotomies, and false analogies in the narrative weaponization model is with types of mis- and dis-information:

Figure 4: Types of Mis- & Disinformation[121]

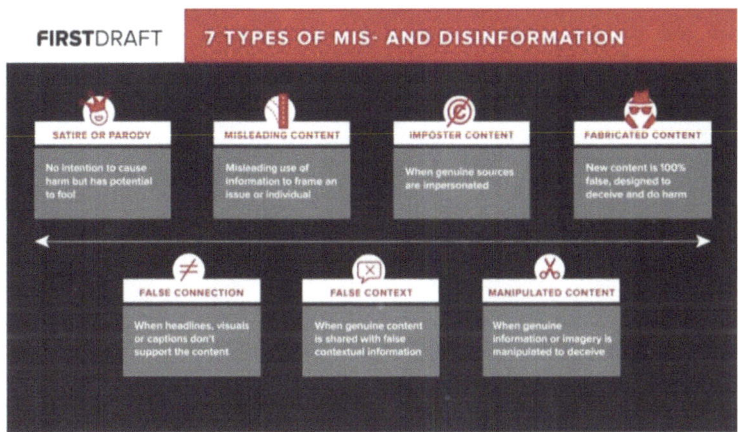

Source: Fake news. It's complicated by Claire Wardle, First Draft

These distinctions are about content, context and connections. A systems approach to the information environment (IE), therefore, takes account of these differences. As an initial step, characterizing the IE in terms of linkages among systems, subsystems, and actors in OODA loops can help map the production and impact of weaponized information.

In this rendition, OODA's "Act" produces information that creates subsequent impact as the information becomes ingested by sentient actors (can include bots, artificial intelligence, etc.) through "Observe... Act" cycles:

---

[121] "Disinformation," Resource Centre on Media Freedom in Europe, posted on October 1, 2019, https://www.rcmediafreedom.eu/Dossiers/Disinformation.

Figure 5: Systematically Mapping Weaponized Information

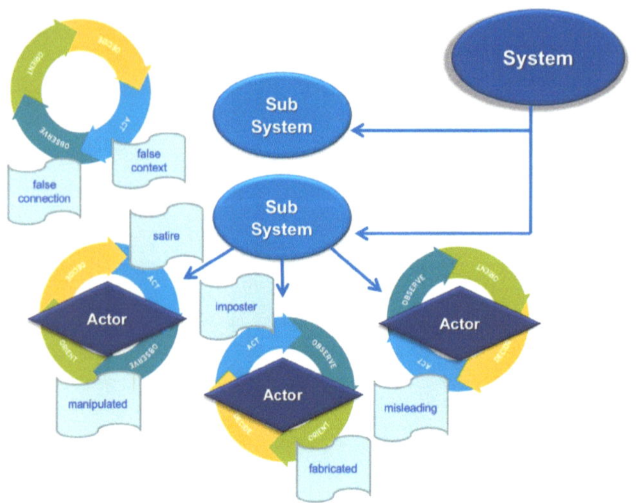

The OODA Loop can be treated as an open system because Observation admits "outside" information and unfolding interaction with the environment.

Now we take a look at some data from Hamilton 2.0 to illustrate Russia's narrative and test it as a weaponized narrative.[122] Another analytical source with which to corroborate this information is EU vs Disinfo.[123]

There is an important difference between what we are about to do as critical thinkers, and what a weaponized narrative's prescription seeks to do to its victims.

We are keeping our observations (the chronology of official Russia information) separate from our orientation (narrative weaponization model). With the exception of the chronology, the Narrative Weaponization Model's components are part of our analytical orientation. Why do we do this?

We take the chronology as observations, not orientation, because our object of analysis is a narrative. Narratives that are not chronological would not fit this definition. This analytical

[122] Hamilton 2.0 Dashboard, Alliance for Securing Democracy, accessed on October 26, 2020, https://securingdemocracy.gmfus.org/hamilton-dashboard/

[123] EU vs Disinfo website, accessed on October 26, 2020, http://euvsdisinfo.eu.

separation allows us to test the fit of the model based on the evidence of what is observed. The italicized words in our synopsis of the model provide the evidence of weaponization.

Russia's Strategic Narrative

We don't have to infer Russia's strategic narrative, thanks to ample studies and evidence. Russia's narrative is a barrage of multiple messages that EU vs Disinfo describes in terms of five types: elites versus the people; threatened values; lost sovereignty or threatened national identity; threatened collapse; and "hahapropaganda."[124] The latter involves joking about evidence. This corresponds to the satire or parody type of mis- and dis-information identified by the Resource Centre on Media Freedom and Europe.[125]

From this credible description, we derived Russia's overall narrative in the following terms. Any state, company, segment of a population, or individual may be inserted into the blank, depending on the desired target:

__________ *is an elitist, incompetent threat to stable Eurasian values and secure identities.*

Next, we look at this narrative for fit as a weapon in terms of Hamilton 2.0's Top 10 Tweets by Retweets, Top 10 Retweets by Likes, and Top Broadcasts (59 in all) between April 15-20, 2020. These are all from official Russian sources, with a few noted follow-on activities.

As in the China case, we have arranged brief descriptions of the Tweets and Broadcast into Maan's Narrative Strategy Model, to show their fit as a weapon, as follows:

Fit as a Weapon (Structure, Re-description, Internalization, Prescription)

- Structure
    - Chronological Sequence
        - Istanbul Mayor Imamoglu criticizes President Erdogan's sudden imposition of a curfew to combat COVID-19

[124] EU vs Disinfo, "5 Common Pro-Kremlin Disinformation Narratives," EU vs Disinfo Website, posted on April 2, 2019, https://euvsdisinfo.eu/5-common-pro-kremlin-disinformation-narratives.

[125] Resource Centre on Media Freedom in Europe Website, accessed on October 26, 2020, https://www.rcmediafreedom.eu.

- Graffiti reported in Chicago blames capitalism for spreading the coronavirus
- Young people in Kocaeli, Turkey, fled in panic upon seeing a natural gas distribution vehicle thinking it was a police van
- 5.3-magnitude earthquake hits California
- Interior Minister of Turkey Soylu to resign for failing to provide adequate notice of curfew
- Subsequent rejection of Soylu resignation by President Erdogan
- Opinions that Soylu's resignation reflects poorly on President Erdogan
- Police officer in Texas escorts a flock of ducklings while guarding Memorial Park
- WHO doubts that patients recovered from COVID-19 are immune
- Fire is extinguished near Chernobyl nuclear power plant (Ukraine)
- WHO does not discount possibility of a second coronavirus wave
- President Trump announces US will halt funding to WHO
- Scientists discover that the coronavirus can survive under 60 degrees
- In Turkey, sea traffic halted due to coronavirus, while dolphins are observed under a bridge
- Will antibody tests be the key to ending lockdowns?
- Feds bailouts will create mass inflation
- First person to survive ICU in a Croydon hospital is discharged
- Why Sanders is wrong to endorse Biden
- War and COVID-19 both kill slowly via humanitarian issues
- 911 call and witness accounts of JFK grandniece and her son's drowning are released
- Will COVID-19 be the end of the EU?
- UFC Sports to return to TV
- Half million New Yorkers will get food relief
- The end of single-use toilet paper?

- Chris Cuomo complains of CNN's hyper-partisanship, then withdraws comments
- 99-year old veteran raises money for UK national health system
- US economy to slowly reopen while cases mount
- Will self-employed in UK survive the lockdown?
- COVID-19 gives Scottish breweries a hangover
- Challenging the New York Times' baseless anti-Russia media attack
- Life in lockdown for Brits living abroad, Himalayas edition
- What is the WHO and who funds it?
- Why are minorities in the UK having high COVID-19 casualty rates?
- Old in and young out—is the UK's exit strategy?
- Oil demand nosedives driving prices to record lows
- US hockey stars to raise charity funds by playing video games, while baseball resumes in Taiwan
- Obesity biggest factor in COVID-19 hospitalizations in NYC, after age
- German police foil ISIS attack on US base
- 106-year old in UK beats COVID-19
- Deceased pedophile J Epstein's co-conspirators are off the hook due to Epstein's secret plea deal
- NYC Mayor challenges the White House
- How did China suddenly become blamed for COVID-19?
- India surpasses France and Great Britain economically
- Increase in volunteers in the UK during COVID-19
- Journalists sound off on CNN anchor's (C Cuomo) confession of partisanship
- New earth discovered 300 light-years away
- Who benefits from the biggest scandal in the UK Labour Party's history?
- Lockdown could force UK pubs to ditch 50 million pints
- Will coronavirus cause more babies or divorces?
- Non-corona virus patients are afraid to get treated due to fear of infection

- Police score "own goal" by breaking social distancing rules
- Chris Cuomo fake quarantine?
- Social workers are not protected from COVID-19
- Cancer patients face delayed treatment
- Assorted sports reporting
- US President and NY Governor continue to spar over COVID-19
- UK lockdown is debated; nation's mental health is affected
- Russian students are stuck in the US under a US State Department program without Russia's consent
- US economy is in standstill; antiviral drug company's stocks soar
- UK launches investigation into minority death rates from COVID-19
- Who were the first 10 doctors to die of COVID-19 in the UK?
- UK gives preferential treatment to patients with higher likelihood of survival
- Londoners don't understand the 3-week lockdown extension
- US plan to open economy to give states much leeway
- Romanian workers who do not meet normal immigration standards are flown into UK as labor
- US car manufacturers facing mounting stress
- Faulty cause and effect & selective evidence
- Capitalism as the cause of pandemic projects a broader contextual image of frustration in the US
- Inadequate curfew notification as the cause of Soylu's resignation, rejected by Erdogan, sows speculation about Immoglu's motives and frames Soylu as a potential rival to Erdogan
- Perceived Turkish police presence as cause of fleeing youngsters reinforces distrust of Erdogan government
- Trump's halt of WHO funding is set up as the cause that connects to subsequent health-related issues (as effects)

        - Government policies create multiple problems—inflation, divisiveness, unfairness
        - COVID-19 may cause: the EU's demise; humanitarian crises; chronic unemployment; medical treatment backlogs; disproportionate deaths among minorities

- Redescription
    - Artificial dichotomies & false analogies
        - NATO countries are incompetent at handling COVID-19, while Russia can be trusted
        - US undermines the WHO even as the pandemic is expected to last longer, while Russia understands the issues
        - Americans blame their own capitalist system for making coronavirus worse, while Russians understand what works during such crises
        - Police are needed in the US to guard public parks, while Russian police fight real threats
        - Ukraine has ongoing environmental problems near Chernobyl [subsequent media coverage amplified the scope of the fire as worst since the 1986 nuclear explosion][126]
        - US and UK are politically divided; Russia is united
        - Social workers in US and UK are not protected; social workers in Russia are protected (implied)
        - Conservative thinkers are responsible; liberal thinkers are not to be trusted
        - Eurasia is on the rise; Western Europe and the Americas are in decline
        - Coronavirus lockdown in US and Western Europe is debated; Russia's lockdown is understood by the people

[126] Olga Shylenko, "Fires in Chernobyl Exclusion Zone are Still Getting Closer to the Reactor," *Science Alert*, posted on April 14, 2020, https://www.sciencealert.com/fires-in-chernobyl-exclusion-zone-have-now-reached-the-ghost-town-of-pripyat.

- Internalization
    - Take responsibility and blame others
        - US capitalism preys upon its own people and allies, rather than solving global problems
        - US will cause deaths elsewhere by not supporting the WHO
        - Turkey (NATO ally of US), is to blame for its own incompetency with respect to coronavirus curfew
        - Ukraine has not taken sufficient precautions to prevent another Chernobyl disaster
        - US is blaming China for the coronavirus and not supporting the WHO, which deserves blame itself
        - Sanders the supposed revolutionary endorses Biden the ultimate insider—blame the rigged US political system

- Prescription
    - Identify and comply with narrative
        - The increased uncertainty of information during the COVID-19 pandemic increases targeted audiences' identification with Russia's narrative. Audiences that are less accustomed to faulty information are more vulnerable to the arguments with anti-Russia conspiracy bias. In addition, the absence of active journalism that scrutinizes government-provided information prevents disclosure of relevant information.
        - Follow on exaggerations reinforce identifying with the pro-Russia narrative. Such as, "Russia Bringing Masks and Gloves to Estonia, USA Bringing Javelin Missiles," despite the fact that Estonia paid for the protective equipment from China.[127]
        - Follow on military activities also send a message: reenactment of a World War II battle in the Estonia-Russia border town of Ivangorod on "Defender

[127] VPK News, "Russia Bringing Masks and Gloves to Estonia, USA Bringing Javelin Missiles," *VPK News*, April 2, 2020.

of the Fatherland Day" intend to deepen emotional attachment to Russia, at least among non-citizen Russophones in the Baltics.

Narrative Analysis

Structure

Russia's narrative as chronology permits inexhaustible insertions of selective evidence, and faulty cause and effect. Selective evidence promotes faulty cause-and-effect thinking. Our snapshot sample begins with observations that set up subsequent conclusions about Turkey, the US, and Ukraine.

First, the Istanbul Mayor's criticism of President Erdogan's surprise imposition of a curfew can be tied to later observations that "prove" the government is out of touch with its people: Kocaeli youth fleeing an apparent police presence and the Interior Minister's offer of resignation rejected by the President. Adding that sea traffic is halted by the ongoing crisis of COVID-19 amplifies a message of incompetent elitism.

Second, graffiti in Chicago blaming capitalism for spreading the coronavirus can be connected to a subsequent observation that conveys selfism capitalism: President Trump announcing the halt of funding to the WHO.

Third, the fire extinguished in Chernobyl, Ukraine, is providing Russia's state-run media such as RT and Sputnik opportunities to reveal contradictions and coverups from Ukrainian state officials.[128]

Overall a chronological sequence that excludes counter-evidence simplifies cause and effect circularity. The result is, believed truth.

Re-description

Artificial dichotomies and false analogies reinforce the faulty cause-and-effect thinking above. There seldom is an example of Russia doing some good, without a rival doing lots of bad. The

[128] "Watch Ukrainian Firefighters Battle Massive Flames Near Disused Chernobyl Nuclear Plant," RT Website, posted on April 12, 2020, https://www.rt.com/news/485596-chernobyl-forest-fire-radiation; "Raging Chernobyl Wildfires Raise Risks of New Radiation Contamination," *Sputnik News*, published on April 13, 2020, https://sputniknews.com/society/202004131078936938-raging-chernobyl-wildfires-raise-risks-of-new-radiation-contamination.

openly debated ways that NATO and its partners deal with COVID-19 is manipulated as incompetence and self-interest. By avoiding negative intent with respect to Russia, a misleading contrast implies that Russia does better. To sharpen the contrast, "the entire ecosystem of Russian disinformation" fabricates content.[129] Furthermore, false context can use genuine information made available by cyber theft from Advanced Persistent Threat 28 (APT28).

Timely re-description of the narrative at memorable moments and in vulnerable locations can expand the narrative. A calendar of events for each target may be constructed. In February, for instance, two days offer multiple opportunities to Russia.

February 23, Defender of the Fatherland Day, offers multiple opportunities. This year, reenactment of a World War II battle in the border town of Ivangorod physically demonstrated Russia's commitment to Russian-speaking peoples. Psychologically, the event re-described that commitment to the city of Narva on Estonia's side of the border, which is 80% ethnic Russian and only 48% Estonian by citizenship.[130] Russia's narratives consistently describe those who express non-Russian identities as Russophobes (see EU vs Disinfo's "Disinfo Review" for notorious examples each week).[131]

February 18th, on the last day of the Battle of Debaltseve, Ukrainian forces were forced to withdraw against more and better equipped Russian forces.[132] Russians went on to assume control of over 7% of Ukraine territory. This year, Russian-backed proxies assaulted Ukrainian positions, three days before the 5th anniversary of the Minsk II Agreement that called for a ceasefire. The periodic physical escalation maintains Russia's foothold inside Ukraine to strengthen its voice against NATO or EU integration.

How well the narrative becomes internalized among various groups requires knowledge of contexts. In Ivongorod and Narva, Russian media reportedly is consumed mostly by older people, while the youth view local websites.[133] In Ukraine, Russia's re-description of its

---

[129] Ali Dukakis, James Gordon Meek et al., "Facing Coronavirus Pandemic, US Confronts Cyberattacks," *ABC News*, published on March 17, 2020, https://abcnews.go.com/Health/facing-coronavirus-pandemic-us-confronts-cyber-attacks/story?id=69653329.

[130] Josh Rubin, "NATO Fears That This Town Will Be the Epicenter of Conflict With Russia," *The Atlantic*, published on January 24, 2018, https://www.theatlantic.com/international/archive/2019/01/narva-scenario-nato-conflict-russia-estonia/581089.

[131] EU vs Disinfo, "Disinfo Review," EU vs Disinfo Website, accessed on October 26, 2020, https://euvsdisinfo.eu/disinfo-review.

[132] Mark Raczkiewycz, "Looking Back at the Battle of Debaltseve," *The Ukranian Weekly*, published on March 8, 2019, http://www.ukrweekly.com/uwwp/looking-back-at-the-battle-of-debaltseve.

[133] Ilya Koval, "Narva: The EU's 'Russian' City," *Deutsche Welle*, published on May 26, 2019, https://www.dw.com/en/narva-the-eus-russian-city/a-48878744.

seizure of territory as something else—protecting Russians in eastern Ukraine—helps maintain an active armed conflict. That rules out NATO membership.[134]

Internalization

Taking responsibility to blame others is a straightforward matter in the preceding examples of Turkey, the US, and Ukraine. Maintaining the relative blame away from Russia is more nuanced, depending on the aforementioned local context. The importance of internalization to Russian narrative strategies depends on the usefulness of the targeted population for various issues.

For instance, that the Erdogan government is distrusted by the Turkish people for the moment is useful to making Erdogan more susceptible to Putin's influence regarding Turkish and Russian operations in Syria. A longer-term internalization of pro-Russia feeling in Turkey is neither necessary nor realistic anyway.

With respect to dividing US opinion via polarized narratives that highlight partisanship (e.g., Lee Camp on Sanders endorsing Biden), that's enough to draw attention to a divided NATO. Internalizing domestic or international blame is useful for Russia even if Russia receives much of the blame. What is important for Russia is that the divisiveness proliferates Russia's narrative.

The case of Ukraine, and the Baltics, is where internalization of blame can generate lasting effects using the same issue. Territorial disputes are not easily forgotten. So, getting local segments of the population to care about domestic corruption and incompetence is feasible in non-NATO countries where there are territorial issues. Believing that Russia is less corrupt and more competent is problematic, but irrelevant if enough blame can be heaped on the targeted state and if security assistance is not credible. Russian President Putin continues to blame Ukrainian President Zelensky for failure to implement Minsk II, even as Russia wages proxy war as the "serial violator" of that agreement.[135]

---

[134] Sim Tack, "Kyiv's Push to End Eastern Ukraine's Conflict Risks Prolonging It," *Stratfor Worldview*, published on March 4, 2020, https://worldview.stratfor.com.

[135] I24 News, "Putin Urges Ukrainian Counterpart to Uphold Minsk De-Escalation Agreement," I24 News, published on February 14, 2020, https://www.i24news.tv/en/news/international/europe/1581700184-putin-urges-ukrainian-counterpart-to-uphold-minsk-de-escalation-agreement; John E. Herbst, "Russia, Not Ukraine, is Serial Violator of Ceasefire Agreement," Atlantic Council alert, published on June 21, 2017, https://www.atlanticcouncil.org/blogs/ukrainealert/russia-not-ukraine-is-serial-violator-of-ceasefire-agreement.

Prescription

The increased uncertainty of information during the COVID-19 pandemic can be exploited to increase targeted audiences' identification with some of the many negative aspects of Russia's narrative. Audiences that are less accustomed to faulty information may be more vulnerable to arguments of an anti-Russia conspiracy. Some NATO members such as Latvian leaders pride themselves in educating the public on pro-Russia media bias.

The presence and absence of active journalism can be exploited. Journalism that scrutinizes government-provided information promotes more disclosure of relevant information. That information can be bent with false context, content and connections. Without active journalism, narratives have less competition in getting people to identify themselves as pro-Russia/anti-NATO-EU and to take action.

Finally, exaggerations can reinforce identifying with the pro-Russia narrative. Such as, "Russia Bringing Masks and Gloves to Estonia, USA Bringing Javelin Missiles," despite that Estonia paid for the protective equipment from China.[136] Add to this blame that the pandemic will be persistent, and that targeted actors are incompetent to handle the problem. That messaging expands opportunities to exploit subsequent mal, mis and disinformation.

Overall, Russia's information spewage fits the Narrative Weaponization Model, but not for the same purpose as in China's case. China's purpose is zero-sum, as in an OODA Loop applied to a life-or-death dogfight. You must buy into China's narrative, or China's narrative will buy you out. There is no particular reason to join China's narrative, and no acceptable alternative to joining China's relationships on China's terms. The narrative justifies itself. Which is precisely the subversive purpose of China's narrative: to replace critical orientation with ideological belief. Observe & Orient fit the narrative; Decide & Act are compliant.

In Russia's case, the purpose of weaponizing a narrative is to distort the decision-making Loop, rather than to collapse it into a belief (China's case). We discern this intent in each stage of the model and in the impact on OODA decision-making. The impact is to Persuade and Compel, and Dissuade and Deter. Our final section details how this combined effect works and recommends how to defeat it.

[136] VPK News, "Russia Bringing Masks and Gloves to Estonia, USA Bringing Javelin Missiles," *VPK News*, April 2, 2020.

Combined Effects Strategy

Russia's narrative works on a target audience through a "distort and influence" mechanism:

- Distort how a target Orients on its environment: the narrative's lens/perspective deforms what the target Observes[137]
- Influence the will and capability to Observe: this reorientation affects how the target Decides and Acts

Figure 6: Combined Effects Strategy

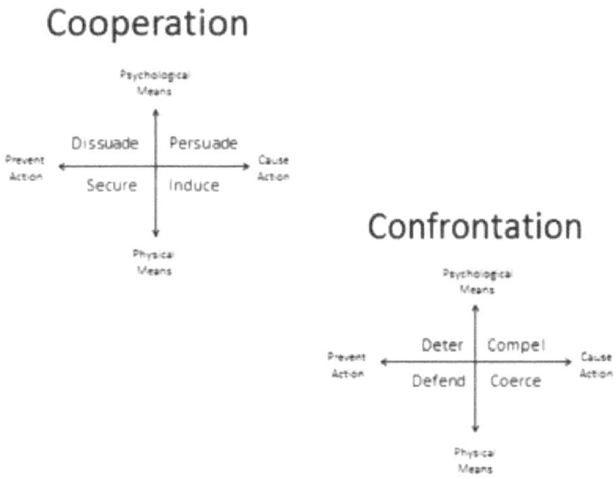

As depicted in Figure 4 above (and detailed in the China case),[138] combined effects strategy uses psychological means and physical means to prevent and cause action. These cooperative and confrontational effects range diagonally from "Dissuade" to "Coerce" and frame four spectra of opposite effects:

[137] Nasim Mansurov, "What is Lens Distortion?" *Photography Life*, updated on July 5, 2020, https://photographylife.com/what-is-distortion.

[138] See chapter 3 of this book.

Cooperative:

Dissuade (Ds) ——————— Persuade (P)
Secure (S) ————————— Induce (I)

Confrontational:

Deter (Dt) —————————Compel (Cp)
Defend (Df) ———————— Coerce (Cr)

Each effect can be categorized in general terms such as Diplomatic, Informational, Military, Economic, and Social (DIMES). I include the latter because the US routinely ignores it, to our repeated disadvantage. While China's narrative attempts to Induce positive conclusions about China, Russia's narratives focus more on negative effects that produce more opportunities to divide rivals and partners.

Orienting on observations this way can inform decisions and actions about how to anticipate and create effects. In the competitive world, psychological and physical means can create synergistic, superior combinations of effects.

From this information assault, official Russia seeks to persuade and compel, and dissuade and deter behavior. This combined effect is powerful and flexible across many contexts. How does the narrative influence will and capability this way?

The logic of targeting will and capability is as follows:

- Assure and intimidate an audience's will, in order to persuade and compel, respectively
- Enhance and neutralize an audience's capability, in order to dissuade or deter, respectively

Here are corresponding examples from our Hamilton 2.0 sample that fit this logic:

a. Assure an audience's Will... to Dissuade

Example: Russia protects Russians... to dissuade you from being part of EU or NATO.

b. Intimidate an audience's Will... to Deter

Example: Russia protects Russians... to deter NATO from intervening in domestic affairs or expanding its membership.

c. Enhance an audience's Capability... to Persuade

Example: Russia provides you help... to persuade you to align with Russia.

d. Neutralize an audience's Capability... to Induce

Example: COVID-19 is neutralizing EU capability... to induce you to believe that COVID-19 will compel EU's dissolution.

The above examples, when combined, can be synergistic. Dissuasion and persuasion complement one another to the extent a target cannot be aligned both with the EU and Russia. Deterrence is necessary to maintaining those two effects below NATO's threshold of a significant response. Inducement adds to all three preceding effects.

Three recent examples reveal how the psychological effects of Russian narratives combine with the physical effects of kinetic warfare in different ways.

1. Georgia: Coerce and Compel

Russian support of separatists in Abkhazia and South Ossetia coerced a five-day war with Georgia in 2008. The victory compelled Georgia into accepting Russian forces in both regions, which Moscow recognized as independent. Russia's continued occupation is a breach of the Ceasefire Agreement. The majority of the world's countries consider Abkhazia and South Ossetia to be Georgian territory.

Today, the basic strategy is to exaggerate the danger of further Russian military and diplomatic measures against Georgia to coerce Tbilisi into complying with Moscow's interests.

Narrative warfare in Georgia includes Russian (and Chinese) disinformation about the Lugar Lab in Georgia. The lab, controlled and run by Georgian health professionals, has led diagnostic tests for COVID-19 and is providing medical advice to Tbilisi authorities. In 2018, Russian Defense Ministry alleged that 73 volunteers died in 2015-2016 as a result of volunteering there.[139] In 2020, The Russia Foreign Ministry, in remarkable congruence with official China statements, charged that the US uses the labs to develop bio-weapons close to Russia's borders.[140]

2. Ukraine: Coerce and Compel

Following pro-Russia President Viktor Yanukovych's refusal to sign the Association Agreement with the European Union in 2014, massive demonstrations caused him to flee Ukraine. This sudden loss of Russian influence prompted Russian forces to invade and occupy Ukraine's predominantly ethnic Russian Crimea region. Moscow orchestrated an information campaign and referendum for secession to justify annexation, instigating a separatist insurgency.[141] This support continues in eastern Ukraine to maintain a divisiveness that precludes Ukraine from joining NATO.

The basic strategy is to maintain a coercive Russian presence to compel Ukraine's acceptance of imposed borders.

Narrative warfare includes stripping Ukraine of support from NATO and especially the US. On a 25 April 2020 joint statement by Trump and Putin, they celebrated the meeting of US and Soviet arms in 1945 on the Elbe River at the end of WWII, in order to "put aside differences": "The 'Spirit of the Elbe' is an example of how our countries can put aside differences, build trust and cooperate in pursuit of a greater cause."[142] Such differences include

---

[139] "Moscow Accuses U.S. of 73 Deaths at Biolab Near Southern Russia," *The Moscow Times*, published on October 5, 2018, https://www.themoscowtimes.com/2018/10/05/moscow-accuses-us-73-deaths-biolab-near-southern-russia-a63094.

[140] B. Alexishvili, "Russia and China Denounce 'Hazardous' American Labs in Post-Soviet States," *Georgia Today*, published on May 1, 2020, http://georgiatoday.ge/news/20943/Russia-and-China-Denounce-'Hazardous'-American-Labs-in-Post-Soviet-States.

[141] Michael Kofman, Katya Migacheva et al., *Lessons from Russia's Operations in Crimea and Eastern Ukraine* (Santa Monica, CA: Rand, 2017), 10–16.

[142] "Joint Statement by President Donald J. Trump and President Vladimir Putin of Russia Commemorating the 75th Anniversary of the Meeting on the Elbe," White House briefing, issued on April 25, 2020.

Russia's ongoing war and occupation of eastern Ukraine. US security assistance to Ukraine appropriated by Congress and halted by President Trump became part of a failed impeachment that played into Russia's overall narrative.

3. US: Induce, Persuade, and Deter

Russia's information inducements (phishing) and persuasion (smearing) via personal email accounts and social media in US Presidential elections is a bipartisan acknowledged fact. The purpose and relative impact, and what is going on to influence the 2020 election, is hotly contested in the US Professor Young Mie Kim's tracking of both campaigns, revealing increased sophistication of a basic Russian tactic: fake identities targeting ideological rivals on divisive issues in battleground states.[143]

Russia's violation of the Intermediate Nuclear Forces Treaty (INF)—continued testing and deployment of prohibited cruise missiles (the 9M729)—prompted the Trump administration to withdraw from the INF. Putin-Moscow's persistent lack of transparency is consistent with Russia's narratives. Any agreement or disagreement is useful if it deters NATO and EU expansion.

The basic strategy is to induce and persuade division in the US and other NATO members, and deter both from increasing military support to frontline states.

Narrative warfare: partisan positions that Russian intervention favored the Democrats *or* Republicans assist Russian inducements and persuasion. Despite domestic polarization on that issue and persistent Russian dis-, mis- and mal-information, Russia has not deterred increases in NATO capabilities and EU expansion. Ad hoc NATO and EU efforts to counter Russia's narratives compete against a Russian campaign that seeks to compensate for relative economic decline.

[143] Young Mie Kim, "New Evidence Shows How Russia's Election Interference Has Gotten More Brazen," Brennan Center for Justice analysis, published on March 5, 2020, https://www.brennancenter.org/our-work/analysis-opinion/new-evidence-shows-how-russias-election-interference-has-gotten-more.

Concluding Thoughts

Russia's narrative warfare is an integral part of its overall combined effect (P Cp Ds Dt):

- Persuade pro-Russia alignment
- Compel beliefs in liberal capitalism's decay
- Dissuade pro-NATO and EU alignment
- Deter NATO intervention

There are, of course, examples of Persuade-Compel-Dissuade-Deter that contradict one another. This would occur when effects are not planned to be combined, but are instead the consequence of separate actions. We should be able to relate to this in the US, where combined arms focuses narrowly on achieving military effects. Add to that another self-inflicted weakness, the unfortunate US policy assumption that warfare starts when deterrence fails.

We hear this sound bite from senior leaders time after time again. Like a re-description. This chapter's synthesis of decision-making, narrative warfare, and combined effects reveals the narrowness of this predominant assumption. The cost of such obliviousness to information warfare is strategic defeat. To prevent that, we need to be in the arena.

Our overall recommendation with regard to Russia's narrative warfare is to understand how actors combine effects in the information environment. This judgment is based on how narratives influence decision cycles to produce a variety of psychological effects.

We close with a practical list of recommendations to defeat Russia's disinformation:

- Try a combined effects approach to cooperation and confrontation using psychological and physical means, and preventive and causative actions; compare this to other approaches you can implement
- De-fragment US strategy where you can: if it's not joint, not whole-of-government, or not whole-of-society (depending on scope of the threat), it's not competitive in the information environment
- Unite effects, not just ways and means: because combined arms is necessary to win battles, but is insufficient to win wars; promote literacy to spot disinformation; private media outlets can do this with daily examples of Russian cyber and

information attacks (we know this will be politicized, but try it—see EU vs Disinfo)[144]

- Our government at all levels needs to model the values in the US Constitution, which unite us; democracy invites disagreement, yet this disagreement is not divisive inside Constitutional processes
- Do not assume that a great power in the information environment is primarily about resources; it's about having a superior strategy relative to an opponent's strategy
- Anticipate that official Russia will exploit opportunities to polarize and divide its perceived threats; pandemics, oil price fluctuations, domestic discontent, addiction to memes, and power vacuums all provide room for narratives to take hold.

The fact that slaughter is a horrifying spectacle must make us take war more seriously, but not provide an excuse for gradually blunting our swords in the name of humanity. Sooner or later someone will come along with a sharp sword and hack off our arms.[145]

– Carl von Clausewitz, On War, Book IV, Chapter XI

The fact that disinformation pervades society must make us take information warfare more seriously, but not provide an excuse for relegating the battle of ideas to kinetic victory in the illusion that war is only violence. Sooner or later someone will come along with a powerful narrative and erase our values.

– Thomas A. Drohan

---

[144] EU vs Disinfo Website, accessed on October 26, 2020, https://euvsdisinfo.eu/news.

[145] Carl von Clausewitz, *On War*, translated by Michael Howard and Peter Paret (Princeton: Princeton University Press, 1976), 260.

Chapter 5

Narrative IS Strategy: Influence Operations in Afghanistan

Paul Cobaugh

The intent of this chapter is two-fold: first to demonstrate that narrative-centric influence can succeed when constructed and disseminated properly; second to highlight the key components of the formula that we use at NS, Narrative Strategies, to guide narrative construction, which Dr. Maan mentions in the introduction to this book: N=M+I+C+S, or Narrative equates to meaning plus identity plus content plus structure.[146]

Here's a short "cheat sheet" for the formula, which will guide this chapter:

Meaning

Narratives do not necessarily tell the truth; they give *meaning* to a succession of events or facts (real or otherwise). That does not imply that narratives involve patent dishonesty, although they may. It does mean, however, that when a narrative is presented based on the art and science of narrative, it does not allow the audience to derive their own meaning. The narrator(s) controls this.

Identity

Literally, *who* someone or some group is. All people and groups, families, tribes, clubs, nations, religious entities, etc., have specific identities unique to them. Within a group, not all members are precisely the same but they have shared "layers" of identity.

Content

The facts, *pieces of information* (true or not) the narrative or its stories are built around. As Dr. Maan tells us in *Plato's Fear*, narratives are more fundamental than stories: a narrative

[146] Ajit Maan, *Plato's Fear* (Washington, DC: Narrative Strategies Ink, 2020), 20–25.

gives meaning to the information included in the stories that rise out of it.[147] The content of a narrative thus dictates the content of the stories that are pulled out of this narrative.

Structure

The *way* the content is presented is the form or structure of the narrative. The most recognized Western structure is the one outlined by Aristotle in his *Poetics*: that which has a beginning, a middle, and an end.[148] Not all cultures share this structure, particularly outside the Western world.

Influence, by definition, is dimensional and the majority of the national security community, especially within DOD, operates via linear planning and execution. In fact, human beings tend to be "wired" as linear thinkers more often than not. Think of this as the old "left brain/right brain" concept that suggest most people are more engineer types than the "artsy," creative type. Though some science has found that brain activity on left or right sides may not be accurate, it is true that there are "types" such as analytical or creative thinking types. Regardless of brain scans, most of us fall into the analytical category. It has been my experience that traditional linear thinkers and dimensional thinkers see the world very differently or, let's say, are simply wired differently. This makes teaching narrative even more difficult. For this reason and others, I learned that telling a story via the employment of key narrative principles was not only more successful professionally but worked its same magic in teaching and mentoring.

Story I: Influence Without Narrative

These stories or rather narratives intend to convey the meaning of the lessons learned as an IO (Information Operations) practitioner during my yearly Deployments to Afghanistan 2009–2013. The reason that I became involved with Narrative Strategies and felt compelled to share

---

[147] Ajit Maan, *Plato's Fear*, 16–18. Dr. Maan uses the analogy of a tree to make the distinction between narratives and stories clearer: "Think of a tree with a large network of underground roots. The roots are the narrative. The soil is the environment that either nourishes or prohibits seeds from germinating. The tree that we see above ground is the story, with many branches, that gets formed the way it does because of the soil it is rooted in."

[148] Aristotle, *Poetics*, 1.7, 1450b25-30.

these lessons is, tragically, that narrative principles as a tool of influence have not been, nor are now taught to military influence practitioners. Even though the word narrative is tossed around frequently in staff meetings and on documents it is overwhelmingly misunderstood.

I learned narrative strategy and tactics OJT, on the job training, from personal experience in a combat zone, and by trial and error methodology. It wasn't until retirement and meeting Dr. Maan in the beginning stages of our Think/Do tank, Narrative Strategies, that I learned that there is a whole body of research and academic rigor associated with my trial and error strategies and tactics. The following, first of three stories, is about IO, Information Operations, which is influence without narrative and lays the foundation for why narrative is essential to success.

To lay the groundwork for this first story, I must explain a few basics for those not intimately familiar with US Military Operations. First, to discuss narrative as applied to US Military Operations, it is important to note that the US Military operates on three basic levels: Strategic, Operational, and Tactical. For this piece I'll speak briefly to the Operational—essentially one AO (Area of Operations with Afghanistan being the example)—and mostly the Tactical, referring to a specific piece of the Operational. I will also carefully avoid all classified references, only speaking about the role narrative played in some planned IO strategies.

My first Afghan deployment, beginning the summer of 2009, was spent working across the spectrum of Strategic, Operational, and Tactical levels. I was posted to Bagram Airfield but had responsibilities planning and executing IO campaigns for several areas of the country where our TF, Task Force operations, were ongoing, and also for the country as a whole. My primary focus, however, were the East, South, and Northern areas.

While there were some IO successes in this initial deployment, overall, we, The US military, failed to actually "touch a nerve" with Afghan "locals" or adequately explain what exactly the US or the nascent government in Kabul was trying to do. We could explain or highlight specific acts in disparate Provinces, partially stave off negative Taliban IO, and highlight successes, but ultimately, we were in a reactive mode, simply reactively feeding the Public Affairs "news cycle." Our desired effects of empowering a "toddler" government and of influencing rank and file Afghans to have confidence in and/or join that government, I would have to admit, were relative failures. Even worse was that we did not negate Taliban activity and recruitment at the height of the "fighting season."

Failure and mediocre results are not acceptable outcomes, especially in support of our USSOCOM TF, United States Special Operations Command Task Force. Already scheduled to return next year, I vowed in the 7 months before my next deployment to do a real deep dive on the area of the country I would be working in, the east.

The answer to improving performance was not merely improving processes that had succeeded but also identifying the demonstrable gaps in what we had failed to do. The answer, though simple to see in hindsight, was far more difficult to master in the short timeframe prior to deploying again. Time is always limited in a normal, hectic pre-deployment, training cycle. Prioritizing what to focus on in the limited free space in our training schedule left room for one topic only. Fortunately, we chose culture, which led to story-telling and not the standard broad-brush military overview. We tracked down a specialist in the matter, who had acquired his knowledge while on the ground in Afghanistan, during the Soviet War period. He had supplemented his education during the ensuing years digging through old British archives for their extensive historical operations in the region.

At first glance, these two topics appear unrelated, but truth be told, one does not exist without the other. I and my colleagues had all but failed the previous year in one of the first imperatives of the Special Operations world: *we had failed to adequately understand our environment*. Secondly, *we had failed to tell a story (narrative) to a "storytelling" culture*, a story that would explain the meaning of our operations, and why it mattered, to locals.

First, let's look at the story-telling gap. IO campaigns built primarily on reacting to events, by default cede the initiative to the enemy. The best that can be achieved is that the "bad guys" do as little harm to the IO campaign as possible. The little proactive work we'd done was largely centered around "getting ahead of predictable events," such as Ramadan attacks, imminent operations in a specific area, etc., and feeding the "Public Affairs cycle." To make matters worse, much of our effort was focused on explaining operations primarily to Western audiences with Western terminology. Afghan audiences were often at a loss to make sense of these explanations due to language and cultural differences.

Story II: Pashtuns and Storytelling

Honor and Shame

With the above said, we began our next tour with the intent to build an overarching Narrative for all of Afghanistan, although at the time we called it a story, supported by the old military mainstay of "themes and messages." Building overarching narratives is always an excellent opportunity to highlight the connection between understanding local culture and telling a story that resonates with a target audience. As we settled into a "deep dive" on Afghan culture it became all too apparent that Afghanistan, the region, the International community, and select areas in Afghanistan, all have significantly different cultures. Afghanistan alone is a complex fabric of culture, religion, and ethnicities. For example, the US military, much like the US government, had spent much time post 9–11 learning about Islam. In the execution of messaging, talking only about Islam in Afghanistan is as productive as trying to discuss every single subject in the West through the lens of Christianity. There are too many sects, cultures, and local customs to touch an audience with a single narrative. Generic messaging is just plain ineffective to most audiences and results in "talking at" rather than "talking with" the selected target audience.

It is also important to add another note regarding the link between narrative and culture as it pertains to Afghanistan. Narratives, as we have seen, generate stories. Storytelling in Afghanistan, regardless of ethnicity but especially among Pashtuns, is an art form and one of the most significant threads of the cultural fabric. Narrative is critical to any IO strategy, but in Afghanistan, in particular, telling a story is a powerful, connective influence tool.

As most of my second deployment was at the Tactical level, in far eastern Afghanistan— Khost Province to be exact—I focused my pre-deployment education on rural Pashtuns, since they dominate the region. Rural Pashtuns live by an honor code called Pashtunwali (the way of the Pashtun), which they see as nearly synonymous with Islam. For experts there are distinct differences between these two terms, but to a rural Pashtun those differences are immaterial. Understanding this led me to a crucial realization: *Narrative is about meaning, not facts or truth.* Now that I was aware of this, I knew how I would shape my narrative.

As Pashtunwali was the filter rural Pashtuns viewed life by, I determined that the central tenet of my narrative would revolve around the issue of honor or absence thereof, which is at Pashtunwali's core. The name of both my IO campaign and my narrative thus became "Honor and Shame."

"Honor and Shame" was actioned under the umbrella of a narrative that highlighted the all-important tenets of Pashtunwali, which regulates daily life. It is a complex code designed to maintain the honor of individuals, their families and their tribe, sub-tribe, clan, and sub-clan, or Khels. While not all the caveats of Pashtunwali were necessarily productive in supporting a national government in Kabul, they were all productive in stabilizing resistance to a form of the Taliban trolling the valleys of eastern Afghanistan. For example, reinforcing the power of the "first among equals" at the tribal level meant that any act committed by the Taliban, HIG, HEZB-E-ISLAMI GULBUDDIN, or the Haqqani group that usurped local tribal governance would be highlighted as "shameful." Shame is a powerful coercive weapon when properly utilized against those beholden to the constraints of Pashtunwali. Conversely, highlighting the "honor" of individuals that protected their tribes, clans, or Khels against dishonorable Taliban fighters ignoring Pashtunwali served to empower the code as well. The de facto outcome was that strengthened traditional tribal structure became a stalwart defense against the Taliban, denying Taliban fighters safe haven in more villages and valleys than prior to employing the "honor and shame" strategy.

This employment of a culturally attuned narrative strategy, my second tour in Khost province demonstrated beyond a doubt for me, is the only way to reach an audience, using the methods, content, and nuances that they would employ themselves. "Honor and Shame" was a sub-narrative to the overarching Operational and Strategic messaging employed at the National and International level. At the beginning of that second tour, the dictate from HQ in Kabul had been to message to get local populations to respect and participate in the national government. Our campaign demonstrated to my local commander that the IO campaign in conjunction with our CT, counter-terrorism operation had stabilized the local area to the point where they could in fact pay attention to the national government in Kabul.

Lesson learned: Employ narrative, understand and employ cultural techniques, and recognize that CT missions alone cannot do the whole job.

Story III: Adjusting to a New Environment Where Multiple Ethnicities Play Major Roles

Criminals and Terrorists

With this powerful new non-kinetic weapon proven, I vowed to employ it in similar fashion in following tours. As luck would have it, my following tours were again at the Tactical level and focused on northern Afghanistan. Repeat tours in the same location provided me the opportunity to see longer term results, rather than a single application as I'd experienced in Khost.

In pre-deployment training for my following tours I again dove deeply into understanding northern Afghanistan and its significantly different cultural makeup from what I'd seen in the east and south. While I'd hoped to use a similar approach to "honor and shame," I quickly learned that the complexities of the north would require a different approach and a different narrative.

In 2011, much of the north was far more stabilized than the rest of the country and this was especially true regarding Mazar-i-Sharif, or MES, as it is known in military circles, which is in Baghlan Province. The hinterlands of the north, from the Iranian border to the mountainous regions in the far northeast, Kunduz, and other significant pockets, were however still very much at war from different types of Taliban. The most prominent were IMU (Islamic Mujahidin of Uzbekistan) Taliban, both Tajik and Pashtun. Their pragmatic alliance was often held together by sheer force of dominant IMU leadership, since cultural differences were deep.

This was also the time frame when Reintegration was on the rise in the north, especially among Tajik and Pashtun fighters weary of war and mostly on the losing end of fighting. In the midst of the harsh winter months in the northern mountains, weariness, hunger, and being hunted nightly took a heavy toll on fighters.

Generally speaking, IMU fighters are ideologues and not as open to reintegration as their Tajik and Pashtun colleagues. The latter tend to be more pragmatic and often consider themselves every bit as much insurgents and radical as Islamists. As previously noted, there is also no love lost between these unequal elements. The Uzbeks (IMU) were more often than not better educated both secularly and religiously, had better fighting skills and training, and looked down on their Pashtun and Tajik fighters disparagingly. IMU fighters also tended toward leadership positions, which they used to further dominate what they considered "lesser."

Again, analysis provided me with what was to become the core of my northern Narrative. As always, one of the first rules of warfare is to "divide and conquer." The natural divisions between the three main components of the northern resistance, exacerbated by the weariness of being on the losing end of a long war, were rife with opportunity to further split the insurgency and encourage more Reintegration. It is important to note here that Reintegration, or at least the theory of negotiated conflict resolution, is a natural course for Pashtuns by way of a Jirga/Pashtunwali system. This will become important as we go further into the northern IO strategy.

"Criminals and Terrorists" became my northern IO strategy for the ensuing campaigns. Yes, it's an odd name for a strategy, but the logic, based on cultural and situational analysis, is sound. In the complex north there is a generalized secularism that does not exist in the east and south. Even in Uzbek communities there is an aversion to the heinous terrorist acts nearly always attributable to IMU fighters. These fighters, although preferring to be called insurgents, are commonly seen by locals as terrorists and therefore deprived of any honor or respect. While most people in the north see the Taliban as insurgents, there is a reluctant view of them as at least somewhat behaving as soldiers rather than terrorists.

The core of the narrative and my strategy thus focused on both proactively and responsively labeling all IMU fighters as "terrorists" in media and personal engagement, while labeling both Tajik and Pashtun Taliban as "criminals." This is the "divide and conquer" I spoke of earlier. It allowed for some positive developments in the northern "battle-space."

Firstly, it contributed to increasing the natural rift between Tajik, Pashtun, and Uzbek fighters. Since "terrorists" and especially IMU terrorists don't or very rarely Reintegrate, it "cut them out of the herd," segregating them further from the Tajik/ Pashtun fighters, who were oftentimes brutally dominated by IMU commanders.

Secondly, Pashtun and Tajik fighters splintered further over domestic issues in the villages and valleys where Tajiks were more favored by government assistance than Pashtuns.

Pashtuns in the north, unlike other parts of the county, are ordinarily seen as the lowest rung on the social ladder. Tajik Taliban stealing the paltry government assistance from Pashtun villages and homes, from Pashtun fighters' families, also exploited the natural divisions. Using the media to highlight these acts triggered the natural dishonor dynamic of Pashtuns, demanding that they restore their honor, disrupted so publicly by their Tajik colleagues. In fact, Pashtuns in the north have a much-checkered history, but this is another story entirely.

Thirdly, and as noted above, reintegration is a natural method of conflict resolution for Pashtuns operating within the bounds of Pashtunwali. Using a narrative and IO efforts to label all non-IMU fighters as "criminals" rather than "terrorists" opened the door to Reintegration by Pashtun fighters, as well as some Tajik fighters. One can fathom rehabilitation with criminals, but none with terrorists. So long as all fighters were labeled terrorists, the Reintegration door was wedged firmly closed to non IMU fighters. In the north, with most of the population sadly familiar with IMU terror against citizens, they had been all too ready to buy into the IMU being permanently labeled as terrorists.

As for the use of the labeling systems as narrative, native media with my guidance was ready to support the campaign. The advantage lay in using what locals perceived as true, responsible, and honorable. The IO effort mostly lay in shaping local media to run with the concept that increased Reintegration by "criminal" Pashtun fighters was somewhat honorable in light of exploitation by Tajik fighters and condemnation of IMU "terrorists." Military successes against IMU "terrorists" were highly publicized and generated increased support to Afghan National Forces (who received most of the credit). The local media onboard as our "credible messengers," delivering and amplifying the "truth" albeit shaped by our focus, further validated culturally shaped and delivered narrative.

Narrative is at the core of all messaging: the good ole themes of messages each support different versions of the narrative. Like any good story or book, there are multiple and ongoing themes woven into the narrative. The actual thread of that weave are the messages themselves.

Conclusion

Here is what you should take away from this chapter.

I have told you three stories about how I learned the absolute requirement to employ narrative principles as the core of all influence campaigns. I learned the hard way, by trial and error, with many poor results and good results until I began to create my campaigns along the lines of what we, at Narrative Strategies, would later consolidate in our equation: N = M + I + C + S. Those of you reading this book don't have to do it the hard way. This book, the variety of stories within it, and the brilliance of my co-authors describing intricate pieces of influence, are templates for success.

I have written a great deal on other occasions about how the USG/DoD and the IC in particular are failing at influence. This book can and should be put to use as a teaching tool or as a "how to" manual of sorts. The key, however, will be to break the current operational paradigm of our national security community, which is to talk an idea to death. Narrative requires narrators and ongoing conversations with audiences. It fails when it is only reactive, what most call "counter-narratives." Like football, you must play both offense and defense and must always have a game plan, equipment, well-trained players, and a coach who can run the whole team in real-time.

The bottom line is: you can succeed. But to do so, you must put in the work, the training, and play every minute of the game.

Image via Pukhtoogle[149]

[149] Pukhtoogle website, accessed on October 26, 2020, http://pukhtoogle.com. We kindly thank Pukhtoogle for authorizing NS Ink to print this image.

Chapter 6

Myths, Memory and Ethnic War in the Balkans: Weaponizing the Kosovo Battle Narrative

Aleksandra Nesic, Ph.D.

Between the fear that something would happen and the hope that still it wouldn't, there is much more space than one thinks. On that narrow, hard, bare and dark space a lot of us spend their lives.[150]

— *Ivo Andric*

Introduction

One of the most prominent anthropologists and scholars of culture, Edward T. Hall famously proclaimed, "Culture hides more than what it reveals, and strangely enough, what it hides, it hides it most effectively from its own participants."[151] For conflict analysts, national security professionals, war scholars and practitioners alike, separating culture from conflict or conflict from culture could be a grave mistake, yet much of the international community still grapples with the conundrum of understanding the complex connection between the two. Lack of understanding this ubiquitous nexus and thus responding adequately to the local context where culture-conflict pathology exists often makes the impossible a reality.

History is filled with examples where in the *making-of* a culture (or a nation) immeasurable violence and suffering occurs, and often in some of the most intimate of settings—families, neighborhoods, tribes and the like. The sheer carnage is difficult to comprehend by those intervening from the outside of said cultural contexts, rendering the post-conflict stabilization and reconciliation efforts that much more ineffective. Preventing conflicts from happening or escalating often also fails to the lack of understanding of the local context/populations vulnerable to mobilization and weaponization. Balkans is one such example where understanding the root causes and local dynamics of the conflict communities

[150] Ivo Andric, *The Bridge on the Drina* (Chicago: University of Chicago Press, 1977), 49.
[151] Edward T. Hall, *The Silent Language* (New York: Anchor Books, 1973), 29.

still puzzles much of the international diplomatic, military, humanitarian and development professionals. To that end, this chapter contributes to this important volume one narrative of the Balkans that is often overlooked, undermined or altogether dismissed, but that carries past into present and is a powerful determent in the future of the region.

Winston Churchill said that the "Balkans produce more history than it can consume"[152] and much of the history surrounding the Battle of Kosovo is more than what this paper can digest. Nevertheless, given the ongoing crisis in the Balkans, specifically between Serbia and Kosovo, the region continues to hang on the edges of repeating its tragic past. Thus, examining the ontology of the Balkans through the lens of the mythical 1389 Battle of Kosovo narrative is timely. It is after all the narrative that weaponized and mobilized Serbs into war against Bosnian Muslims (1992-1995) and Kosovo Albanian (1998-1999) populations. And more critical perhaps is that this narrative continues to be used by adversaries such as Russia and China, who are increasingly more aware and skilled at weaponizing any and all narratives in an attempt to influence and shape international relations as they see fit.

Historical Context: The Making and Unmaking Yugoslavia

The South Slavic Kingdom of Serbs, Croats and Slovenes became Yugoslavia after a coup which led to royal leadership in 1929. The post-World War II socialist Yugoslavia, led by Josip Broz Tito continued to use the term "Yugoslav" as a means to foster federalist sentiments and in opposition to ethnic nationalism. Tito sought to maintain Yugoslavia as a federal system that accommodated and maintained a mosaic of different ethnic, religious, cultural and linguistic groups. Joseph Rothchild emphasized the almost unbelievable diversity of ethnic groups that Yugoslavia brought under one state, "By virtually every relevant criterion—history, political traditions, socioeconomic standards, legal systems, religion and culture—Yugoslavia was the most complicated of the new states of interwar East-Central Europe, being composed of the largest and most varied number of pre-1918 units."[153] Maintaining political balance and diffusing ethnic tensions was the only way for Yugoslavia to survive, and this

[152] Charlemagne, "Arrest and Revival," *The Economist*, June 2, 2011.
[153] As cited in Vesna Pesic, *Serbian Nationalism and the Origins of the Yugoslav Crisis* (Washington, DC: United States Institute of Peace, 1996), 1. Original passage is in Joseph Rothschild, *East Central Europe Between the Two Wars* (Seattle: University of Washington Press, 1974), 201.

peculiar maintenance hinged mainly on the interdependence of Serbs and Croats, the country's two largest national groups. Tito's Yugoslavia was a successful socially engineered nation, where this mosaic of different identity groups maintained peaceful co-existence for several decades. "Bratstvo i jedinstvo" (Brotherhood and Unity) was the *modus operandi* of the Yugoslav narrative that was maintained for as long as Tito lived.

Leaving no successor, Tito's death in 1981 brought to surface political rivalries for the successor from each of the five republics of Yugoslavia. Federalism in the country inspired nationalistic sentiments among the political leaders in Serbia, Croatia, Slovenia, Macedonia, Bosnia and Herzegovina, as well as within the two semi-autonomous provinces, Vojvodina and Kosovo. Slovenia's secession from the federation prompted the notion of separating national interest among the rest of the republics in the early 1990's—a precedent that set in motion a war that is considered one of the worst in European history since World War II. While Slovenia's secession was peaceful, Bosnia and Herzegovina posed the greatest threat to any prospects of peaceful dissolution. This is so because Serbs, Croats and Serbo-Croats lived there, alongside with Bosnian-Muslims and Bosnian-Serbs, and because both Serbia and Croatia had historical pretensions to Bosnia's territory. In addition to the geopolitical factors that defined the conflict, ethnic and religious differences among the groups shaped the discourse of the war and are powerful drivers behind the regional affairs today.

Serbian religious identity is closely tied to Eastern Orthodoxy, Croatian identity is tied to Roman Catholicism, and Bosnian identity to Islam. Maintaining peaceful coexistence between these groups was possible during the socialist-federal regime of Josip Broz Tito, when religious affiliations were highly bureaucratized and their importance minimized under the narrative of the *supranational* Yugoslav identity. With the exception of Slovenes, none of the other national groups lived within clearly defined borders (physical or psychological) inside the federation; most lived within one of the other's "national" territory and almost every one of them was perceived as a threat to another and has felt threatened itself.

Religion fed the nationalistic aspirations of the political elites during and after the breakup of Yugoslavia, and especially during Milosevic's regime in Serbia. Given that no other strong identifier was available to discern the identities of the three groups at the brink of the conflict, religion became a marker that united elements such as ancient hatred, discriminatory political, economic and social institutions, and it legitimized and justified the atrocities that followed.[154] In order for political elites to separate each group from the Yugoslav supranational identity, they embarked on recalling and reawakening historical narratives unique to the development of each groups' cultural and national identity. For Milosevic, the apex moment was the speech he delivered to a minority Serbian population in Kosovo, recalling the infamous 1389 Kosovo Battle. The political power of the Kosovo Battle narrative served its ultimate purpose: weaponize the Serbs in a holy war against the Muslims.

Mythological Narrative: The Battle of Kosovo 1389

Our identities as individuals and as members of groups are defined through the telling and remembering of stories. Real or imagined, these stories shape our understanding of ourselves as heroes, martyrs, triumphant conquerors and humiliated victims. The most dangerous identity is that of a victim. Once we see ourselves as victims, we can clearly identify an enemy. Steeped in our own victimhood, we no longer feel bound by moral considerations in becoming perpetrators.[155]

— Julie Mertus, 1999.

The Battle of Kosovo of 1389 is a deeply embedded event in the collective memory of Serbian people. As evidenced in a 2000 Frontline interview, Nebojsa Pavkovic, the General who commanded Serbian forces during the Kosovo conflict in 1998-1999, shared this sentiment by revealing Serbia's innate connection to Kosovo and its effect:

> I think that the whole world knows what Kosovo means to Serbia. . . . It is its cradle. . . . Serbia is in Kosovo, and Kosovo is in Serbia. Serbian roots are in Kosovo, and everything that is connected to the Serbs throughout the past centuries is there. Every Serb is intimately connected to it.[156]

---

[154] Aleksandra Nesic and A. Berger, "Yugoslavs Die Less: Yugoslav Self-Identity and Violence During Bosnian War," International Studies Association, San Francisco, CA, April 2012.
[155] J. A. Mertus, *Kosovo: How Myths and Truths Started a War* (Berkeley, CA: University of California Press, 1999), 1.
[156] Nebojsa Pavkovic, "War in Europe: Interview with Nebojsa Pavkovic," interviewed by Peter J. Boyer, *Frontline* (February 2000), retrieved from http://www.pbs.org/wgbh/pages/frontline/shows/kosovo/interviews/pavkovic.html.

This rhetoric was unleashed by a speech Serbian President Slobodan Milosevic gave on June 28th, 1989 on the 600th anniversary of the Battle of Kosovo at Gazimestan, where Kosovo Battle is said to have taken place in 1389. Milosevic revoked the heroic moment of Serbs fighting against the Ottoman occupation, in an attempt to psychologically transfer old enemy Ottoman Turks (Muslims) to the new enemy—Bosnian and Kosovo Albanian Muslims. "Never again will Islam subjugate the Serbs" were his intoxicating closing words that marked the next decade of ethnic wars in the Balkans, first in Bosnia (1992-1995) and then Kosovo (1998-1999). His alluring power over the country and propelling Serbs into a collective euphoria in defending their culture, religion and pride against Islam continues to echo today. The new enemy today among some of the most die-hard nationalists are the Muslim refugees passing through and/or settling in the Balkans—this polemic deserves its own chapter.

The Kosovo Battle has been the story told by generations and carefully guarded for centuries. The significance of June 28th serves as the critical site for the generations and inflections of affective bonds among Serbian people and their connecting roots to a date on the calendar named Vidovdan. Vidovdan, St. Vitus Day, falls on June 28th and is considered one of the most important days on the calendar of Orthodox Serbs. On June 28th, 1389 Kosovo Battle occurred; on June 28, 1914, Bosnian Serb Gavrilo Princip retaliated against the occupying forces of Austro-Hungary and assassinated the Austrian Archduke Ferdinand, setting off World War I. June 28th, 1948 marked the split between the Soviet Communism and Communism of Yugoslavia. And on June 28th, 2001, after almost a decade of intrastate conflicts that reached every corner of former Yugoslavia and left the international community perplexed at the level of war crimes committed, Serbia's former President Slobodan Milosevic, accused of war crimes against humanity was finally arrested and extradited to the International Tribunal in Hague.

On Vidovdan in 1389, the Battle of Kosovo took place, a battle which became one of the most potent events in Serbian history, shaping the identity of every newborn for over 600 years and providing a framework for examining the past, present and future of Serbia. Ever since that St. Vitus Day in 1389, the mythological narrative of the battle and the significant events that occurred centuries later seem less of a coincidence than a carefully orchestrated chain of events for which years in between had collapsed. Bieber suggested that the connection of these events to the epic myth of 1389 was not a coincidence, stating, "Conscious human choices to position these events in relation to a quasi-mystical national framework obviously determined their timing. But their cumulative effect has nonetheless been to reinforce and reaffirm the national significance of Vidovdan."[157] Reaffirming this significance serves as a primary psychological grounding principle, it drives participants toward a collectively stable core architype of what is a Serb, what is the essence, *raison d'etre,* of Serbhood.

The space between today and 1389, or 2001 and 1389 or any other year to 1389 each Vidovdan is what Vamik Volkan calls *psychological time collapse*, a concept that explains the process in which interpretations, fantasies and feelings about the past shared traumas (or glories) commingle with those pertaining to the current situation.[158] Each of the events that occurred on Jun 28th since 1389 evokes the feelings of pride, shame, trauma and glory, not as separated but deeply intertwined and conflicting feelings, experienced all at the same time for centuries. Under the influence of a time collapse, people may intellectually separate the past event from the present one, but emotionally the two events are merged. People speak emotionally of such events as if they happened yesterday and not hundreds of years ago.

The Battle of Kosovo itself as told and retold by generations is an elaborate moral play, a toxic mix of heroism, martyrdom, betrayal, and heroic self-sacrifice. It has for centuries supplied central symbolic architypes for modern male Serbian identity. There are three central figures: Tsar Lazar with a Christ-like depiction, who martyrs himself on the Kosovo plain; Vuk Brankovic, the traitor who at the crucial moment withdraws the troops and leaves the overwhelmed and outnumbered Serbian army; and the ultimate hero Milos Obilic. A critical moment that continues to define and shape heroes, martyrs and traitors of Serbhood, was the last supper on the eve of the battle. Tsar Lazar, deceived by Vuk Brankovic, predicts that he will be betrayed by Milos Obilic. During this dramatic moment Tsar Lazar issued a curse upon all Serbs who would not come to the battle, proclaiming:

Whoever is a Serb and of Serb birth,
And of Serb blood and heritage,

[157] Florian Bieber, "Nationalist Mobilization and Stories of Serb Suffering," *Rethinking History* 6, no. 1 (2002): 95-110.

[158] Vamik Volkan, *Bloodlines: From Ethnic Pride to Ethnic Terrorism* (New York: Farrar, Straus and Giroux, 1997), 34–35.

And comes not to the Battle of Kosovo,
May he never have the progeny his heart desires,
Neither son nor daughter!
May nothing grow that his hand sows,
Neither dark wine nor white wheat!
And let him be cursed from all ages to all ages![159]

The original form of the curse as told through oral history first appeared in 1845, nearly five hundred years after the Battle, as part of the collection of Serbian folk songs recorded by Vuk Karadzic. That chilling curse, those intoxicating words are what generations and generations of Serbian children memorized and proudly performed during school recitals, words that still pierce through school walls and shake the core of Serbian people. The curse is carved on the Gazimestan monument, cementing a reminder to all—to fight and revenge the Serbian honor even if death is imminent. Although Tsar Lazar knew that the Ottoman army was much more powerful and that the Serbian army would lose in the battle, his message was not a military tactic but a desperate decree to uphold *Serbhood* against the oppressors or face a tragic fate of his dooming words. The next morning, before the battle officially commenced, it is said that Milos Obilic headed to the Turkish camp proclaiming that he had defected from the Serbs and abandoned the Tsar. He did so in order to gain access to Sultan Murad who led the Ottoman army. While kissing Sultan's feet, Milos murders Sultan with a hidden dagger, sacrificing his own life as dying Murad orders Milos' execution. Both Tsar Lazar and Sultan Murad were killed on that day, but the Ottoman army was larger in numbers and the Serbian nation succumbed to its rule for the next six hundred years.

Interestingly, what bares little significance in the collective memory and the historical narrative of Serbia is that the actual fall of the Serbian nation occurred eighteen years prior to the Battle of Kosovo, during the Battle of Maritza in 1371. Since 1371 a number of battles were fought against the Ottomans, and one of them was the Battle of Kosovo. What is so significant in the narrative of the Battle of Kosovo, however, is the occurrence of the symbolic narrative of cultural and religious defeat, one that produced a much more disastrous future

[159] John Matthias and Vladeta Vuckovic, translators, "Musich Stefan," *The Battle of Kosovo: Serbian Epic Poems* (Athens, OH: Swallow Press, 1987).

than the Ottoman rule itself. The audacity of Tsar Lazar's curse on the eve of the Battle of Kosovo called to heroically defend culture and religion of the great nation that predated him, an emotional outcry for the loss of the old, glorious past. Under Tsar Dusan and Milutin, who reigned before Lazar, Serbian culture thrived and flourished; Serbia was militarily strong and culturally even stronger. In order to understand the significance of this battle and its effects on the collective memory of the people today, one must look at the role that the Serbian Orthodox Church played before, during and after the Ottoman rule. One must confront the mythical path set up by the Church as the only path on which all Serbs are to walk together.

The identity of Serbian culture is firmly integrated in the national religion that was established in the 12th century. The Grand Prince Stefan Nemanja, the founder of the Serbian state reigned during the early 1100's and along with his son Saint Sava, brought the Eastern Orthodox Church to Serbia and set it in the service of the nation. It was under the first national Church that basic educational and cultural establishments were born and most of the first monasteries and churches were founded in and near Kosovo, thus making Kosovo a critical religious, diplomatic and cultural cradle of Serbia. When Kosovo and Serbia fell into the hands of the Ottoman Empire in 1389, the only entity that could save the nation which was fearfully facing Islamization was the Church. The Church continued its existence throughout the Ottoman rule, carrying forward the unity of people. While some Serbs converted to Islam, and while the Serbian Orthodox Church occasionally and for short periods of time fell under the jurisdiction of the Ottoman rule, most of the time it was independent and continued to lead spiritual unification, healing the wounds of the victimized nation and promoting courage in the face of the occupiers. And because of its close association with the 1817 uprising against the Ottoman rule which finally freed the Serbs, the Church became inextricably linked with Serbian national identity.

Milosevic's famous speech "Never again would Islam subjugate the Serbs"[160] backed by the Serbian Orthodox Church provided the space for the collective psychological shift to occur and opened the channels for the rise of violent forms of nationalism. Milosevic's call for unity under the slogan "*Only Unity Saves the Serbs*" (in Cyrillic "Само Слога Србина

[160] Slobodan Milosevic, televised public speech delivered in Kosovo on June 25, 1989.

Спасава") dates back to the 12th century when it was first inscripted on a cross by St. Sava. In less than two years from Milosevic's speech, time collapsed and collective paranoia took over the nations' collective consciousness and ability to reason. Religiously inspired national myths ignited what Hedges calls the "collective amnesia" of the people in war.[161] The stage was set for a new battle, not a Battle *of* Kosovo, but a Battle *for* Kosovo. The new battle that will forever stand as one of the worst moral crimes that a nation's government committed, the crimes of ethnic cleansing.

The importance of religious institutions supporting mythological narratives of glorious past cannot be undermined. Given that the Kosovo Battle narratives' primal importance was to establish what is a Serb, Serbian nation, i.e. *Serbhood,* making it sacred and saintly was only possible by the aid from the highest spiritual guides, Partriarch Pavle. As religious authority, he supported the narrative that Serbs must fight for what is theirs (referring to Kosovo) which in turn gave credibility for the atrocities that followed. A photograph taken in 1995 on June 28 shows Patriarch Pavle with Radovan Karadzic and Ratko Mladic behind him, both indicted for war crimes during the Bosnian war (1992-1995). Karadzic was the president of Serbia during the war in Bosnia, Mladic was the commanding general of the Serbian forces. In 2016, the International Criminal Tribunal for the Former Yugoslavia (ICTY) found Karadzic guilty of genocide, war crimes and crimes against humanity and sentenced him to 40 years in prison. In 2017 Mladic was found guilty of the same crimes and sentenced to life in prison.

Narrative Past, Present, Future

The mythical narrative of the Kosovo Battle and Ottoman occupation surrenders itself to several central themes carried through the centuries by the Serbian Orthodox Church: Serb victimization, oppression, sacrifice, struggle, revenge, and nationalist religion to complete the discourse. It is visually expressed in iconography that permeate people's homes and educational institutions, it is found in the volumes of oral history memorized by generations of schoolchildren, it is sang in folk as well as popular songs. It keeps the national spirit alive and it unites Serbs at times of national crisis. It provides a framework by which Kosovo Battle

[161] Chris Hedges, *War is a Force that Gives Us Meaning* (Philadelphia, PA: Perseus Books, 2002), 46.

memory becomes an organizing psychological principle around firmly established archetypes of identity. It also reminds generations and inspires the link between medieval Serbia that guided the people through unimaginable century-long hardships until finally they became free from occupation and established a sovereign nation-state. The psychological message of the narrative ultimately set the stage and prevailed in the nationalist ideology and rebuilding of identity through the collective past traumas and glories.

This mix of social trauma and glory echoes through generations, providing the building blocks of Serbian national identity. Ivan Colovic calls this the "folklorization" of current history that transforms "national history into popular literature and mythology."[162] Noel Malcolm describes the epic surrounding the battle as a "totem or talisman of Serbian identity" that represents the "permanent connective tissue that imbues Serbs with the feeling of national identity."[163] Bieber notes that the Battle of Kosovo myth serves the purpose to explain, contextualize, and justify a multitude of developments since the emergence of Serbian nationalism in the early nineteenth century.[164] This process is seen in other places where political leadership and ideologues contemporize the past and historicize the present. By eliminating the time gap between past events and present ones, collective emotional response is that much more potent and vulnerable to weaponization. Volkan's *time collapse* concept explains this development as a rather limited interpretation of history that eliminates unbiased analysis of events and perpetuates pre-judgment, as sometimes, the past is dormant for generations, but may be awakened under specific political conditions.[165] Milosevic's speech woke up that past and glorified it, selecting a specific event, precisely the narrative which fit into a collective need for group identity in the time of national crisis. Portraying Serbia as a heroic and holy nation through the manipulation of history, political ideology of the 90's emancipated dormant events of the past.

---

162 Ivan Colovic, *Politics of Identity in Serbia* (New York: New York University Press, 2002).
163 As cited in P. Lugar, "History and The Effects of the Kosovo Polje Mythology," Master's Thesis, Lafayette College, PA, 1992, retrieved from http://www.dtic.mil/cgi-bin/GetTRDoc?AD=ADA437497.
164 Florian Bieber, "Nationalist Mobilization and Stories of Serb Suffering: The Kosovo Myth from 600th Anniversary to the Present," *Rethinking History* 6, no. 1 (2002): 95–110.
165 Volkan, *Bloodlines*, 34–35.

When multiple generations of Serbs are drawn together by the Kosovo epic mythology, a set of what Julie Mertus called "national truths" develop.[166] Mertus suggested that cultures have a set of "national truths" that affect the collective behavior of a nation, which are "events that people believe to be true and may, in fact, not be factual at all."[167] She recognized the problem when leaders manipulate particularly malignant strains of national truths aided by inaccurate and distorted media reports and deteriorating economic and social conditions, suggesting that "facts are rarely the driving force of human behavior. In terms of their bearing on ordinary human lives, experience and myth are far more persuasive and influential than factual truth."[168] Presently, the world is filled with such actions by both state and non-state actors, using mis/disinformation in order to influence and change behavior of populations to radicalize, extremize, mobilize and weaponize populations. Understanding how narratives work in creating, recreating and determining one's identity trajectory is critical for those intervening, preventing and/or countering such efforts from adversaries.

Conclusion

The link between the Kosovo past and Kosovo present is evident in current political climate. Although Kosovo's independence was rectified in 2008 by the UN court and recognized by the 86 UN member countries, the Serbian government is reluctant to accept such change. Accepting the change would symbolize accepting the defeat of 1389; it would mean losing its cradle of cultural and religious property, and ultimately losing every aspect of what it means to have a national narrative that determines who Serbs are, and by extension who their friends and foes are. Holding tightly to the *Kosovo is Serbia* framework, the myth of victimization and courage keeps the flames alive in Serbia's quest to not lose its core archetype.

What is critical to note is that this narrative is well known to the Russian state, which uses elements of it to promote loyalty, brotherhood, Christian Orthodoxy and Slavic unity. On a number of occasions, Russia has sent their highest religious leaders to Serbia to show solidarity, it has utilized NATO bombing of Serbia to end Kosovo conflict as a method to

[166] J. A. Mertus, *Kosovo: How Myths and Truths Started a War* (Berkeley, CA: University of California Press, 1999), 65.
[167] Mertus, *Kosovo*, 67.
[168] Mertus, *Kosovo*, 69.

drive Serbia away from joining European Union (EU) and NATO, and more critically it continues to support the narrative by accepting Serbian volunteers to fight on their side in eastern Ukraine since the annexation of Crimea. A small group of Serbian volunteer fighters have gone to Donbas to "support Russian brothers" because "that is what Tsar Lazar would have wanted us to do."[169] Russia's *"Crimea is Russia, Kosovo is Serbia"* policy continues to drive political and ideological links between the two nations and those willing to support the narrative.

For all interested in or working in the Balkans region, gaining a deeper understanding of the nexus between the Kosovo Battle narrative and Serbian identity is critical in understanding the population's thinking and behavioral patterns. Narratives are inextricably linked with ones' identity but without understanding the deeper psychological and existential connection between the two, our efforts at producing effective messages will continue to fail. This case illustrates one example in the ocean of international conflicts where the cultural narratives play penetrating role in how conflicts develop, how people get polarized, and ultimately how ethnic cleansing and genocides occur. If those intervening from the outside of cultural contexts do not have adequate understanding of what "culture hides," we will never be able to achieve the kinds of effects to combat the logic of ethnic exclusivity and persecution, in the Balkans or anywhere else.

---

[169] Vice News, "Serbian War Veterans Operating in Crimea," *Vice News*, March 9, 2019, https://www.youtube.com/watch?v=pFlLN9E2kcY.

Part III

Stability and Statecraft

Chapter 7

Structuring for Success in Narrative Engagement

Colonel (Retired) Christopher Holshek

In war, moral factors account for three quarters of the whole; relative material strength accounts for only one quarter.

– Napoleon Bonaparte

As a young Army captain stationed in Germany, in 1985, I was privileged to brief Chancellor Helmut Kohl and an entourage of civil and military officials at a tank range in Grafenwöhr. Over a lunch of field rations, Kohl told me a story I heard from many Germans of his generation—about how GIs gave foodstuffs to his family in the early postwar period. Stories like this, Marshall Plan era "care packages," the "Monuments Men" salvation of Western artworks, and many others, shaped a strategic narrative that made it practically as well as politically impossible for the Soviets to break the will of the allies, despite a massive disinformation program backed by immense hard power. This strategic narrative was further rooted in the widespread presence of Americans in European neighborhoods over generations.

Between 1945 and 1989, as many as 20 million American military personnel, civilian employees, and family members spent part of their lives working and living in Europe.[170] People got to see how Americans really were and not just what the media told them—and the walk largely supported the talk. Beyond pop culture, this interpersonal, democratic level of connectivity between populations and not just elites—long before Facebook—was what really made NATO more than just a political or military alliance. Its resiliency and strength were grounded in a transatlantic community of whole-of-society pluralistic values and a common collective identity of liberal democracy and free markets. Practical as much as political, it helped "the corrosive power of freedom," as NSC-68 termed it, eventually expose the inadequacies of communism to meet rising expectations—and brought down the Berlin Wall.

---

[170] See the author's "Legacies of the U.S. Presence in Germany," *Amerika in Rheinland-Pfalz*, edited by Winfried Herget (Trier: Wissenschaftler Verlag, 1996), 149–60.

As in many of today's conflicts, the Cold War involved a competition of ideas between great powers—it was a case study of U.S. military's role in the balance and alignment of soft and hard power in execution of Cold War strategy in narrative strategy. Although decisive, the main difference is how "community relations" activities then were supporting actions that are now becoming leading activities. Still, the U.S. European Command required every soldier and civilian to spend their first two weeks in-country in the "Headstart" program that taught basic survival language skills and a primer on the country and culture in which they served—including a list of "do's and don'ts" to stay in good standing with their hosts. The program emphasized that implicit to their mission was how they served as ambassadors for their country, providing a moral as well as material bulwark against Soviet expansionism. Other than that, Americans there were left on their own to just be who they were. In many respects, it was one of the most successful examples of community-based, civil-military peacebuilding in history.

Given the continuous, people-centric rivalries of identity and ideas, involving a complexity of great powers, non-state actors, and illicit syndicate networks of the 21st century, DoD, the Joint Force, and especially the Army must embrace the cognitive realm of conflict and competition with the same seriousness, conscientiousness, and systems integrity as it has the episodic, state-on-state and force-on-force conflicts of 20th century conventional combined arms warfare in the largely physical domains where it has been more at home. In fulfillment of Napoleon's dictum, the U.S. foreign and national security establishment must expand its wholesale as well as retail understanding of its craft and learn to integrate moral and material power institutionally as well as operationally, from the bottom up as much as the top down.

Expanding from the Material to the Moral

To prevail in the uncertain, dynamic, and ambiguous strategic and operating environment described as a "continuum of competition," what the Army calls "Unified Land Operations" call for more holistic, integrative leveraging of broad, whole-of-nation capabilities for success in the moral as well as material spaces—because the centers of gravity in this continuum have increasingly shifted more from the material to the moral. In response, the Army has also developed the concept of Multi-Domain Operations (MDO) to drive institutional change "to ensure that the intellectual precedes the physical in the development of the future force, enabling the United States to win in competition and conflict in the future."[171]

At the same time, however, the Army must address its incapacities for MDO support to Joint All-Domain Operations (JADO) to "prevail in competition, ...penetrate and dis-integrate enemy anti-access and area denial (A2/AD) systems and exploit the resultant freedom of maneuver to achieve strategic objectives (win), and force a return to competition on favorable terms."[172] In a larger sense, it is about staying on the winning side of a constant, multidimensional power struggle—power being the demonstrated capacity, ability, or will to change or influence behavior or the course of events.

Because this idea of continuous competition exposes the limitations of the conventional binary notion of conflict that is either war or peace, victory or defeat, the Army must grow its capacities to "actively compete *left* of conflict in order to enable winning *in* conflict."[173] Conflict prevention is application of Sun Tzu's observation that the supreme art of war is to subdue the enemy "without fighting."[174] Regardless, the Army must "expand the battlefield" beyond the largely physical domains of MDO (land, sea, air, space, and information) to cognitive capacities and aggressively pursue their development. At the same time, it must recognize that decisive cognitive factors exist in the totality of MDO. Cognitive force capabilities are as essential to war-winning as combat forces and do not exist merely to set conditions for "victory" in conventional conflict and post-conflict stabilization. While firepower has its own impacts, now foremost among military capabilities are those designed to influence populations and leaders through an effective narrative strategy that integrates moral and material power.

Institutional change begins—but does not end—at the conceptual level. The current era of long-term strategic competition, contested norms, and persistent disorder requires "the seamless integration of multiple elements of national power—diplomacy, information,

---

[171] Lieutenant General Eric J. Wesley, USA & Colonel Robert H. Simpson, USA, Ret., *Expanding the Battlefield: An Important Fundamental of Multi-Domain Operations* (Arlington, VA: Association of the United States Army, 2020), 2.
[172] Department of the Army (DA), U.S. Army Training and Doctrine (TRADOC) Pamphlet 525-3-1, *The U.S. Army in Multi-Domain Operations 2028* (Washington, DC: U.S. Government Printing Office, December 2018), 17.
[173] Land Warfare Paper 131, 2.
[174] Sun Tzu, *The Art of War*, translated by Lionel Giles, The Internet Classics Archive, accessed on October 26, 2020, http://classics.mit.edu/Tzu/artwar.html.

economics, finance, intelligence, law enforcement, and military," per the *National Defense Strategy*.[175] This is regardless of when or where in the competition continuum, and it is nothing new. Competition, after all, "is older than warfare itself; it is the original politics," of which war is merely an extension, entailing a contest of wills that is fundamentally political, human, and psychological.[176] Conflicts since 9/11 have reminded us that, "to wage war effectively, civilian and military leaders must operate as successfully on political battlegrounds as they do on the physical," while "integrating efforts across those battlegrounds is essential to success in war."[177] They also rediscover how "military power alone is insufficient to achieve sustainable political objectives," and that "there are limited means to achieve integration across the instruments of national power," as the capstone *Joint Concept for Integrated Campaign Planning* puts it.[178] Beyond expansion of the physical domains that form most of MDO, this requires a more strident alignment of interorganizational activities prescribed in the *Stabilization Assistance Review* and DoD Directive 3000.05.[179]

The informational element of power is a paramount operational as well as strategic consideration in modern warfare and power competition. "The information domain determines winners and losers and the best weapons do not fire bullets," National Defense University professor of strategy Dr. Sean McFate told an audience of civil affairs professionals.[180] But he was preaching to a minority in the Army and Marines who were already among the converted. Even the *Joint Concept of Operations in the Information Environment* (JCOIE), in an understatement, concedes the U.S. military has "failed to maximize the potential of informational power."[181] It also states the core military problem at hand: "How will the Joint Force integrate physical and informational power to change or maintain the perceptions, attitudes, and other elements that drive desired behaviors of relevant actors in an increasingly

[175] Jim Mattis, "Summary of 2018 National Defense Strategy of the United States of America," Department of Defense, 2018, 4.
[176] Kelly McCoy, "In the Beginning, there was Competition: The Old Idea behind the New American Way of War," *The Modern War Institute*, April 11, 2018, https://mwi.usma.edu/beginning-competition-old-idea-behind-new-american-way-war.
[177] Nadia Schadlow, *War and the Art of Governance–Consolidating Combat Success into Political Victory* (Washington, DC: Georgetown University Press, 2017), 2.
[178] Joint Chiefs of Staff, "Joint Concept for Integrated Campaigning," Department of Defense, March 16, 2018, 4.
[179] "Stabilization Assistance Review—A Framework for Maximizing the Effectiveness of the U.S. Government Efforts to Stabilize Conflict-Affected Areas," Washington DC: Department of State, U.S. Agency for International Development, and Department of Defense, January, 2018.
[180] Christopher Holshek, "2020 Civil Affairs Roundtable Report Roundtable Goes Virtual–and Viral–in Response to Coronavirus," The Civil Affairs Association, May 5, 2020, 2.
[181] Joint Chiefs of Staff, "Joint Concept for Operating in the Information Environment," Department of Defense, July 25, 2018, iii, vii, 7.

pervasive and connected information environment to produce enduring strategic outcomes?"[182]

In order to maintain continuous advantage in the informational environment, the Joint Force must have:

> the ability to understand the perceptions, attitudes, and other elements that drive behaviors that affect Joint Force objectives; the ability to characterize, assess, synthesize, and understand trends of relevant actor activities and their impacts on the information environment throughout cooperation, competition, and conflict; the ability to execute integrated physical and informational activities designed to achieve psychological effects; and, the ability to assess and modify informational power with the same level of competency as physical power.[183]

Information-related capabilities to shape and influence the human geography give the Army, which leads U.S. civil-military operations per Title 10 USC and DoD Directive 5100.01, a decisive advantage.

Operationalizing integrated physical and informational power requires institutionalizing it. Informationally driven MDO and JADO are inherently strategic—from planning to execution. This calls for greater strategic thinking, especially at lower levels of military leadership, to institute the "competitive mindset" the *National Defense Strategy* deems necessary to win modern wars. Strategy, after all, is the "employment of specific instruments of power (political/diplomatic, economic, military, and informational) to achieve the political objectives of the state in cooperation or in competition with other actors pursuing their own—possibly conflicting—objectives."[184] Inherently comprehensive, "strategy seeks to influence and shape the future environment as opposed to merely reacting to it."[185] An update to the Officer Professional Military Education Policy lists strategic thinking and communication as the first of the Joint Learning Activities.[186] This, however, is only a start to solving a systemic problem.

---

[182] Joint Chiefs of Staff, "Joint Concept for Operating in the Information Environment," iii, vii, 7.
[183] Joint Chiefs of Staff, "Joint Concept for Operating in the Information Environment," xi and 35-39.
[184] Harry R. Yarger, *Strategic Theory for the 21st Century: The Little Book on Big Strategy* (Carlisle, PA: Army Strategic Studies Institute, February 2006), 5-6
[185] Yarger, *Strategic Theory*, 5-6.
[186] Joint J-7, Chairman of the Joint Chiefs of Staff Instruction 1800.01F, Officer Professional Military Education Policy, Department of Defense, May 15, 2020, A-A-1.

Beyond Information Warfare to Narrative Warfare

To expand MDO from the physical to the psychological, the Army's view of informational power must go well beyond the conventional approach to Information Operations (IO) of messaging target audiences as a form of firepower. Instead, it must defeat more sophisticated use of information in support of strategic aims by adversaries. "Our opponents mean to fracture our alliances, partnerships, and resolve," noted strategic thinker Huba Was de Czege:[187]

> They intend to influence our home and Allied publics. They mean to create ambiguity, slow our recognition of danger, confuse our policy decisions, and block or misdirect our reactions. This would be a clearer statement of the problems we must address. Just how does the Army contribute to this political, military, and economic realm of international affairs?[188]

While warfighters have learned that contemporary tactical actions have direct political consequences, they have likewise learned that tactical and technical proficiency alone is an insufficient skill set. As military professionals, they must know how to compete on complex human terrain where they have often been overmatched by adversaries with a superior understanding of those skills and that terrain as well as the advantages of cultural interior lines and far greater leeway to manipulate local dynamics to achieve holistic or strategic effects. They must know almost as much about how to maneuver in this terrain as shooting, moving, and communicating to find, fix, and destroy bad guys. This requires as much a change in mindset as an adaptation of new skills sets.

According to Shona Brown and Kathleen Eisenhardt, authors of *Competing on the Edge: Strategy as Structured Chaos*, people and organizations are successful because they've learned to find the edge between structure and chaos that allows for innovation and creative as well as critical thinking at the lowest levels.[189] It also requires just enough discipline to focus on executing a plan along with the humility to adapt it to changing realities. This is why

---

[187] Brigadier General Huba Wass de Czege, U.S. Army (Retired), *Commentary on "The U.S. Army in Multi-Domain Operations"* (Carlisle, PA: USAWC Press, 2020), 17.
[188] Czege, *Commentary*, 17.
[189] Shona L. Brown and Kathleen M. Eisenhardt, *Competing on the Edge: Strategy as Structured Chaos* (Cambridge, MA: Harvard Business Review Press, 1998).

the education of soldiers may, in fact, prove more valuable in an era of strategic competition than just training. McFate, in his book, points out how a strong liberal arts education can help military as well as civilian leaders more effectively deal with complexity, uncertainty, and ambiguity.[190] War, after all, is as much art as science. That ability to navigate in the moral spaces requires a strong sense of identity that is value-based—which is why military education emphasizes it as it does. Value-basing is essential to applied personal, organizational, or national strategy. Values, played out in space and time, provide impetus for identity as well as interests, which in turn inform strategy and policy, and then the actions of organizations and individuals—within as well as beyond our shores.

Despite the often mesmerizing allure of technology, the Army has always been the premier force for human interaction. "Cyberwar's real power in modern warfare is influence, not sabotage. Using the internet to change people's minds is more powerful than blowing up a server," McFate observed.[191] The Army is considering expanding its Cyber Command to an Information Warfare (IW) Command to include IO and IW as well as cyber and electronic warfare.[192] But would it be enough? As with the idea of "competition," the Army lacks clear definition of integrated influence operations. RAND offers one:

> the coordinated, integrated, and synchronized application of national diplomatic, informational, military, economic, and other capabilities in peacetime, crisis, conflict, and post-conflict to foster attitudes, behaviors, or decisions by foreign target audiences that further U.S. interests and objectives.[193]

The same goes for the Army's understanding of "narrative," which narrative strategist Dr. Ajit Maan explains is "the telling of a story in a certain way for a certain purpose. The way is through the process of finding and refining personal and collective identity. The purpose is influence at both those levels. Through narrative we construct our personal and

---

190 Sean McFate, *The New Rules of War: Victory in the Age of Durable Disorder* (New York: William Morrow, 2019).
191 McFate, *The New Rules of* War, 16.
192 Sydney J. Freedberg, Jr., "Army To Build New Info War Force – Fast," *Breaking Defense*, August 22, 2019.
193 Eric Larson, Richard Darilek, Daniel Gibran, Brian Nichiporuk, Amy Richardson, Lowell Schwartz, Cathryn Quantic Thurston, *Foundations of Effective Influence Operations: A Framework for Enhancing Army Capabilities* (Santa Monica, CA: RAND, 2009), 1, 201.

cultural identities. Ideas and beliefs result from those identities, and actions follow."[194] To further explain its composition, Maan employs a formula: Narrative=Meaning+Identity+Content+Structure (N=MICS), discuss in greater detail in other parts of this book.[195]

What differentiates narrative warfare from information warfare is that narrative warfare focuses on the strategic struggle over the meaning of information, rather than "information dominance" itself. Less about facts or truth, it is more about beliefs they may underwrite. Narrative strategy recasts IW with the necessary strategic mindset to unlock the full potential of narrative warfare, which, in turn, provides the operational conceptual context for integration of information-related capabilities and the more focused development of related skill sets. In an operating environment that involves as much art as science, understanding the strategic narrative and corresponding families of narratives at work is vital for prevailing in the contemporary competition continuum. Narrative strategy and warfare, which employs cognitive visualization tools (versus physical operations measures and evaluations) to see, understand, and engage cognitive spaces, is still not integral to the current concept of MDO.

Narrative Power through Engagement

The Army may already have an integrative, unifying concept to operationalize integrated informational and narrative power in the *Functional Concept of Engagement* it introduced in 2014.[196] In MDO, engagement is "the combination of physical, informational, and psychological actions taken to influence actors' decision making." Because war is "fundamentally and primarily a human endeavor," the Joint Force "must address the cognitive aspects of political, human, social, and cultural interactions to achieve operational and national objectives."[197] Inherently offensive and based in cooperation, engagement expands the competitive space through conflict and return to competition, including gray-zone unconventional or irregular warfare. As a core competency, the *National Defense Strategy*

[194] Ajit Maan, "Narratives are about 'meaning,' not 'truth,'" *Foreign Policy*, December 3, 2015. See also her *Narrative Warfare* (Washington, DC: Narrative Strategies Ink, 2018) and *Plato's Fear* (Washington, DC: Narrative Strategies Ink, 2020).
[195] See Ajit Maan's introduction to this book and Paul Cobaugh's chapter, "Narrative IS Strategy."
[196] U.S. Army, "U.S. Army Functional Concept for Engagement," TRADOC Pamphlet 525-8, U.S. Army Training and Doctrine Center, February 24, 2014.
[197] U.S. Army, "The U.S. Army in Multi-Domain Operations," TRADOC Pamphlet 525-3-1, C-10, December 6, 2018.

prescribes, commanders and statesmen should "offer competitors and adversaries an outstretched hand, open to opportunities for cooperation but from a position of strength and based on our national interests."[198]

The core activity of engagement is relationship-building—regardless of the type of operation and when and where in the continuum it takes place. It is how to gain and maintain access and influence among communities in the non-transactional cultures most U.S. military professionals encounter, and where individual identity is in the context of tribal and family identity. It is an inherently strategic and even generational process that most Americans, being from a largely transactional and tactical culture, have difficulty comprehending. The product, in fact, is the process of building trust—the social currency and strategic and operational capacity required to move things forward in a mutually positive way. As seen during the Cold War, ongoing relationship-building at the ground level is essential to the rooting of alliances and multilateral networks that should remain a key strategic advantage of the United States versus its adversaries. As the African proverb goes, "when you walk alone, you go faster; when you walk together, you go farther." At the same time, engagement has immediate and lasting impacts on the ground. A form of civil and cognitive reconnaissance, it is essential to synthesizing civil information with military considerations that is key in Joint Intelligence Preparation of the Operational Environment.

Engagement builds more than partner institutional and indigenous governance capacities and joint, interorganizational, and multinational (JIM) networks to see, understand, shape, and influence the cognitive environment. The strategically conscientious conduct of engagement not only grows the strategic and operational capital for response to unanticipated non-linear attacks and hybrid warfare. That same capital enables strategic and operational optionality, empowering those who have it to set the conditions and call the shots in competition and concentrate efforts on exploiting strengths instead of covering weaknesses—playing offense more than defense. Maximizing cooperation (friends) and minimizing conflict (enemies) is how to win in competition. This mindset helps reach the layers of identity that successful narrative strategy and warfare can trigger for influence—in other words, it builds

---

[198] Jim Mattis, "Summary of the 2018 National Defense Strategy: Sharpening the American Military's Competitive Edge," Department of Defense, January 19, 2018, 4–5.

narrative power. Strategic land power is at the heart of unified action in competition. It means more than mitigating stand-off influence operations. It means seizing the initiative, lifting the fog of competition, and accelerating decision cycles to win without decisively committing combat forces, as Sun Tzu would have it.

More than applied strategic economy-of-force, comprehensive, continuous, and consistent engagement is a scaled up version of what General Stanley McChrystal termed "collaborative warfare."[199] Joint Publication 3-08, *Interorganizational Cooperation*, describes collaboration as "a process where organizations work together to attain common goals by sharing knowledge, learning, and building consensus."[200] An employment of a strategic narrative of inclusion, a collaborative warfare approach to engagement goes even further to create the extended learning organizations the U.S. and its allies require to stay ahead of the power curve, seize strategic initiative, and shape the competitive space rather than be shaped by it.

"We have to *continually* be countering information warfare and unconventional warfare," former Deputy Commanding General of Army Futures Command (AFC) Lt. Gen. Eric Wesley admitted: "That requires day-to-day coordination among the U.S. military, U.S. civilian agencies, and allies [through] operational headquarters that are conducting competition every single day in an aggressive and rapid manner."[201] It also requires acculturation of a strategic narrative of engagement in the Army's own organizational culture that sees its capacities, capabilities, and activities as inherently offensive and decisive in their own right rather than a "force multiplier." Despite the legal and bureaucratic obstacles, it's a challenge—and an opportunity—the Army can't continuously ignore. "This can't be done agency-by-agency or even country-by-country," Wesley adds: "One of the reasons we struggle with it is we see it as an afterthought. We do it episodically, anecdotally."[202] If the Army does not seriously invest in these capacities and capabilities, then it need not be surprised that it gets what if pays for.

---

[199] As cited in Assad A. Raza, "Collaboration: Key to Successful Civil-Military Operations," *Eunomia Journal*, May 20, 2020.

[200] Joint Chiefs of Staff, "Joint Publication 3-08, Interorganizational Cooperation," Department of Defense, October 12, 2016), I–11.

[201] As cited in Sydney J. Freeburg, Jr., "Fog of Information War: Army Asks Civilians, Allies for Aid," *Breaking Defense*, 25 September 2019.

[202] Sydney J. Freeburg, Jr., "Fog of Information War: Army Asks Civilians, Allies for Aid," *Breaking Defense*, 25 September 2019.

Indeed, combatant and service component commands and their unified action partners must "build campaign plans that integrate, converge, and leverage national elements of latent, indirect, and direct powers" in the highly complex and dynamic environments of especially urban areas of competition and A2/AD.[203] Such politico-military decision-making support requires robust, permanent, and integrated civil-military planning teams at theater and Joint Force commands. This would generate a competition mechanism to obtain civil-military convergence of MDO, interorganizational stabilization, and consolidation of military and security gains into desired political and civil outcomes. Commanders and interorganizational partners require a full range of integrated moral and material options for proactive execution of simultaneous and sequential operations across and beyond all domains. If these capabilities are not optimized at the institutional level, they will most assuredly not be optimized at the execution level.

An instituted strategic narrative of engagement also enables the Joint Force to "outmaneuver an adversary cognitively as well as physically and virtually to deter, counter, and deny the escalation of violence in competition, and defeat the enemy if armed conflict cannot be avoided," as the current MDO concept adds.[204] As such, engagement forces are essentially maneuver forces for decisive action as well as setting conditions in the cognitive spaces that make up expanded MDO and competition. The proof, however, is in the pudding.

Structuring for Success in Competition

To expand MDO from the material to the moral, the Joint Force must have "the ability to organize, train, equip, and maintain organizations that deliberately leverage information and the informational aspects of military activities"[205] and the ability to integrate operations—organizationally as well as operationally. The good news is that the Army provides the Joint Force with most of these capabilities: Civil Affairs (CA); Psychological Operations (PSYOP) and IO/IW; Foreign Area Officers (FAOs); and, Public Affairs (PAO). These forces also have the best access to unified action partners to bring additional (and often more appropriate and

[203] McCoy, "In the Beginning, there was Competition."
[204] U.S. Army, "The U.S. Army in Multi-Domain Operations 2028," TRADOC Pamphlet 525-3-1, U.S. Army Training and Doctrine Center, December 6, 2018, C-10.
[205] Joint Chiefs of Staff, "Joint Concept for Integrated Campaigning," Department of Defense, July 25, 2018, 39.

effective) capabilities to bear. For competition, the Army also maintains numerous security cooperation activities, beyond its overwhelming focus on train-and-equip, to programs such as International Military Education and Training (IMET), the goals of which include establishing "a rapport between the U.S. military and the country's military to build alliances for the future."[206]

Perhaps the most underappreciated institutional advantage the Army maintains for competition is in the activities of its robust reserve forces. The National Guard's State Partnership Program, another highly effective low-budget training and institution-building program, likewise has the relationship-building effect that easily translates into strategic and operational capital. So does the U.S. Military Observer Group, a Joint program run by the Army that provides United Nations field missions with highly impactful staff augmentation and military observers who act as "strategic scouts" and "strategic enablers."[207] In addition to the benefits for readiness and emergency response, the Army Reserve Command's Private Public Partnership (P3) program is a reminder of the reserve component's capacity to leverage America's entrepreneurial, community-focused mindsets and commercial power for competition. Another promising initiative is regionally aligned Security Force Assistance Brigades, albeit focused largely on improving "the capability and capacity of partner nations' or regional security organizations' security forces" to conduct combat operations.[208]

Still, the strategic as well as transactional relationship-building benefits of these programs are unmistakable. The Army would be indeed wise if it vastly expanded its network of liaisons and representatives at multiple government, non-government, and private sector organizations to improve situational awareness and understanding, influence them more, and professionally develop the kind of strategic, collaborative leadership skills it needs to be a more effective force in the 21st century. It need only exploit the programs and infrastructure it already has.

---

[206] Defense Security Cooperation Agency website, accessed on October 26, 2020, https://www.dsca.mil/programs/international-military-education-training-imet.
[207] Christopher Holshek, "America Needs Peacekeeping Missions More Than Ever," *Foreign Policy*, November 10, 2015.
[208] Army Techniques Publication ATP 3—96.1, *Security Force Assistance Brigade* (Washington, DC: Army Publishing Directorate, 2018), 1-3.

Less encouraging, however, is that Army capabilities for competition and engagement in the moral spaces are not as well managed with the same energy and deliberation as its capabilities to conduct major combat operations. An example outcome is that, despite the clear lesson from the Global War on Terror of the need for cultural expertise, the Army still makes occasional effort to recruit among diasporas that provide, beyond language skills, the insider understanding for narrative engagement of foreign populations for CA, PSYOP, IO/IW, or other related specialties above—they are normally guided to assignments in military intelligence. Another is how pre-deployment country, cultural, and intercultural interaction training for ground troops remains uneven across commands, and is often done last-minute. These skills, along with negotiation and mediation, are not considered warfighting skills. And more than fifteen years after DoD Instruction 3000.05 declared stability operations a core military mission equivalent to combat operations, the subject remains an elective course at senior staff colleges.

The main problem is organizational. Nested among disparate commands, components, and functional authorities, with disjointed mission focus, organizational cultures, and force development and management priorities, their institutional disarray complicates the ability of theater, operational, and tactical commands. It is hard enough to calibrate and converge all of this so as to maximize MDO and JADO for competition, let alone integrate moral and material power.

The U.S. Army Civil Affairs & Psychological Operations Command (Airborne) is the best example of both the problem and much of the solution. With the overwhelming majority of DoD engagement capabilities (over 82% of its CA, 83% of PSYOP, and 71% of IO), it is the ideal core for a more robust Army command to manage and deploy integrated information related capabilities, in part because of the unique civilian acquired knowledge and skill sets of its members. Unfortunately, it is an Army reserve organization that should be a multi-component command, to include active component information related capability forces.[209] For Force 2025, USACAPOC(A) is implementing a seven-year "Harnessing Collective Influence" strategy to integrate CA/PSYOP/IO and grow functional specialists and other

[209] Major Assad A. Raza, "True Civil Affairs Integration: From Three Tribes to One," *Eunomia Journal*, October 31, 2019.

human capital in partnership with the private sector and non-governmental organizations. This is good, but not enough.

USACAPOC(A) constitutes 5% of the Army Reserve yet accounts for over 20% of its deployed operations tempo. Continued high demand presents unique challenges for Army and Joint commands that need CA/PSYOP/IO more than ever for competition missions. The Army and Joint Force, however, cannot leverage them short of partial or full-scale mobilization without great difficulty in, for example, negotiating cumbersome Cold War era authorities and budgetary mechanisms. This and USACAPOC(A)'s force, training, and readiness management practices echo the Army's big-war legacy institutional model. Rather than a much-needed operational integration command for CA, PSYOP, and IO/IW, it remains essentially a force provider of small teams and personnel to tactical and operational commands for exercises and operational support. For these and other reasons, USACAPOC(A)—and the commands it supports—are not optimally structured for success in the competition continuum.

And if they are not optimally structured to integrate physical and informational power, then neither is the Army or the Joint Force. Addressing this critical vulnerability calls for changes at the wholesale as well as retail level. For starters, to expand MDO beyond its predominantly physical domains requires institutionalizing an informational, human, or cognitive domain—not simply an extraction from all the others. For General Robert Brown, commander of U.S. Army Pacific, the cognitive domain should not only be a domain, but the most important among them.[210] To integrate military-civilian physical and informational power, the Army must establish an engagement or influence warfighting function, with its own unified command structure and an Army center of excellence. This way, it could organize all the relevant forces and activities, such as security cooperation—with strategic direction from the Defense Security Cooperation Agency—which should maneuver as combined forces do in competition, the same way infantry and armor do in combat.

From top to bottom, the Army must treat the conceptualization, organization, command and control, development, management, equipping, deployment, and employment of

---

[210] Major Kimber Nettis, USAF, "Multi-Domain Operations: Bridging the Gaps for Dominance, Sixteenth Air Force (Air Forces Cyber) newsletter, March 16, 2020, https://www.16af.af.mil/News/Article/2112873/multi-domain-operations-bridging-the-gaps-for-dominance.

engagement forces as seriously as it does combat forces. In addition to their own domain and command, these forces need representation on the Army and Joint staffs—e.g., the Army G9 covers installation management, while the Joint Staff J9 (civil-military operations) comes much closer. In fact, any use of the "9" designation of staff should be for the engagement function and should coordinate all engagement-related forces and activities in the command area of responsibility.

To operationalize moral-material integration and win in competition, the Army must first institutionally converge and calibrate its engagement forces and activities, fostering a superior strategic learning organization of an open society both within and beyond military and national structures. It must seize opportunities to be a greater force for engagement and influence through interorganizational collaboration in national strategic initiatives like the *Stabilization Assistance Review* and the Global Engagement Center. It must build an industrial base in applied social sciences, related individual and organizational learning technologies, and political and civil information management, as well as human terrain mapping and analysis systems. Above all, it must invest in people more than platforms to cultivate strategic and operational capital (including recruiting and talent management), so that the Army can gain and maintain strategic initiative and optionality, win left-of-bang, and preserve blood and treasure—to co-opt the Civil Affairs motto and "secure the victory" in the totality of competition. The Army must show it means what is says and not just say what it means.

Walking the Talk

From organizational, training, material, leadership and education, personnel, facilities, as well as policy and doctrinal perspectives, the U.S. military must recognize, institutionalize, and operationalize its mission as a moral as well as material force. Structuring for success is both a wholesale and retail enterprise. It is continuous as competition and not merely episodic. Like narrative, it is organic and involves life cycles or learning and re-learning. In many ways, there is nothing new here—identity, in fact, is personal and collective values in action, and actions often speak louder and further than words. Seen this way, engagement is an exercise in collaborative leadership by example. Given the amplifiers of social media and other communications platforms, walking the talk is by far the most powerful and enduring way to influence people and communicate the power of ideas in their lives.

While narrative strategy may be mostly top-down, narrative warfare is mostly bottom-up. As far back as my time in Germany, I saw that formal, high-visibility, top-directed events do less than informal, low-profile activities at the community level. That's because they create more enduring bonds and impressions from substantive person-to-person contacts, promoting this increasingly vital aspect of international relations. Building relationships and trust is nothing more than getting people together and kicking off the conversation. Simply juxtaposing people along common lines of interest like education, business, sports, cultural and social groupings (e.g., women, religion), and of course the military, and allowing them to interact freely, has been the most effective formula. As I saw over my years in service, the behavior of especially our younger informal ambassadors, for good and for bad, transcending language and culture, has more impact on the success or failure of our foreign relations than anything else.

The American military and those who wear its uniform must never forget that, regardless of its employment, it is first and foremost an instrument of diplomacy on behalf of the American people. They may, at times, be our only representation to foreign populations and leaders. Another way to think of this kind of interpersonal narrative engagement is as A2/AD in the cognitive or informational domain—as filling the informational gaps of who we are and what we're about and defeating attempts at misinformation and disinformation to the same end. Narrative engagement is best when it is a more conscientious connection of moral legitimacy credibility at home as well as abroad. As an intra-societal organization of citizen-soldiers, the Army is an institutional thought leader in this process. Everything it does that is true to the foundational principles of the Republic it defends makes its moral and material strength and power that much more unbeatable; everything it does to detract from those principles makes it all that much weaker and more vulnerable.

Chapter 8

Rewriting the Narrative: A Path Forward for Policing

Frank G. Straub, Ph.D.

Introduction

We are at a watershed moment in American policing. Last year, 2020, was defined by COVID-19, civil unrest, increases in violent crime, and calls to reform and/or defund the police. To understand the fissures that exist in community-police relations, and to identify a path forward from the crisis, we must consider how we got here. In doing so, we must recognize that many of the underlying factors in the debate are tied to the realities of life for people in socially and economically disadvantaged neighborhoods and to the women and men who are charged with peace keeping—the police. We must also consider the narratives that have influenced discussions around neighborhood violence, community-police relations, and civil unrest.

Narratives generate stories and give meaning to events and occurrences.[211] They are the way we create, transmit, and in some cases negotiate meaning. We organize, prioritize, and order our experiences through narratives. We understand not only the world around us, but also ourselves, through the narratives told by our parents, extended families, neighbors, faith leaders, and political leaders.

The use of strategic narratives by law enforcement at the neighborhood-level provides a foundation on which to build effective dialogue and implement strategies to prevent and control crime, to improve community-police relations, and to generate opportunities for peace keeping—"left of conflict." Operational narrative strategies create windows for law enforcement to influence interpretations of their actions and disrupt the strategies meant to sow civil discord and unrest.

The Challenges of Police-Community Relationships

For many people, who live in socially and economically disadvantaged neighborhoods—poverty, a lack of opportunity, disrupted families, violence, and hopelessness define the

[211] See Ajit Maan, *Plato's Fear* (Washington, DC: Narrative Strategies Ink, 2020), 16–18.

narrative. In poor neighborhoods of color, homicide is ranked among the leading causes of death among young men. Scholars and police chiefs agree that neighborhood violence stems from: gang and drug activity, access to guns, impulsiveness, "disrespect," unemployment, poverty, and persons transitioning in and out of incarceration.[212]

For the last four decades, police departments, challenged by surges in violent crime and calls for quick and decisive action by the public and elected officials, relied on aggressive enforcement narratives and strategies to fight the "wars on crime and drugs."[213] The strong emphasis on *fighting* crime and the dramatic increases in incarceration that resulted, tore a hole in the social fabric of many neighborhoods. Communities of color in particular, suffered from aggressive and indiscriminate police tactics that failed to bring peace and stability to their neighborhoods. Stepped-up enforcement of public ordinances, and the use of stop, question and frisk tactics, increased tension between the police and communities of color, which viewed the tactics as intrusive, oppressive, misguided, and race based.

Overly aggressive police tactics reduced police credibility, particularly in those neighborhoods that needed police services the most. Although the tactics were intended to reduce crime and keep "good" residents safe, the use of the tactics disenfranchised the very residents they were meant to protect. Elijah Alexander, a Yale professor, described police-community interactions in *Code of the Street* in these words:

> In the community the police are often on the street, but they are not always considered to have the community's best interest at heart. A great many residents have little trust in the police. Many assume that the police hold the black community in low repute and sometimes will abuse its members... With this attitude many people are afraid to report obvious drug dealing or other crimes to the police, for fear that the police might reveal their names and addresses to the criminals.[214]

---

[212] Thomas Abt, *Bleeding Out: The Devastating Consequences of Urban Violence. Anda Bold New Plan for Peace in the Streets* (New York: Basic Books, 2019), 51.
[213] Patrick Sharkey, *Uneasy Peace: The Great Crime Decline, The Renewal of City Life, and the Next War on Violence*, (New York: W.W. Norton 7 Company, 2018), 129.
[214] Elijah Alexander, *Code of the Street: Decency, Violence, and the Moral Life of the Inner City*, (New York: W.W. Norton, 1999), 320

Wesley Lowery, author of *"They Can't Kill Us All"* wrote:

> In hundreds of interviews, residents of the North County [Ferguson] suburbs told me heartbreaking stories of arbitrary traffic stops and aggressive street stops and pat downs, emergency calls ignored by police, and the enduring perception that the deaths of black and brown men are neither fully investigated nor solved—especially at the hands of police officers.[215]

The "war narratives" that were advanced during the past forty years have proven remarkably durable.[216] In fact, few observers of American policing would disagree with the statement that police-minority relations remain stressed by ongoing issues. In August 2020, the Center for Court Innovation in New York, released: "Gotta Make Your Heaven: Guns, Safety, and the Edge of Adulthood in New York City."[217] The project investigated the experiences of New York City youth ages 16-24 who were at high risk for gun violence (e.g., carried a gun, been shot or shot at). Youth participants (330) were recruited from three neighborhoods with historically high rates of gun violence when compared to the city as a whole—Brownsville (Brooklyn), Morrisania (Bronx), and East Harlem (Manhattan). Among its findings, the project concluded:

- The majority of youth expressed extreme dislike and distrust of law enforcement, with an overall sense that the police were a negative force in their communities. This lack of trust stemmed from three primary concerns: being stopped for low-level offenses, feeling the police were not addressing serious crime and violence, and sensing a lack of care for people in the community.
- Participants felt that police treated gang members and youth from the projects as less than human, "criminals," "demons," and "animals." They also made specific connections between their poor treatment by the police and their race.[218]

---

[215] Wesley Lowery, *"They Can't Kill Us All:" Ferguson, Baltimore, and a New Era in America's Racial Justice Movement* (New York: Little, Brown and Company, 2016), 45

[216] Sharkey, *Uneasy Peace*, 130.

[217] Rachel Swaner, Elise White, Andrew Martinez, Anjelica Camacho, Basaime Spate, Javonte Alexander, Lysondra Webb, and Kevin Evans, "Gotta Make Your Own Heaven: Guns, Safety, and the Edge of Adulthood in New York City," Center for Court Innovation, August 2020, https://www.courtinnovation.org

[218] Swaner et al., "Gotta Make Your Own Heaven."

In the words of Marc Lamont Hill, "to be Nobody is to be vulnerable. For the vulnerable, it is the violence of the ordinary, the terrorism of the quotidian, the injustice of the everyday, that produces the most profound and intractable social misery."[219]

The current moment provides an opportunity to reconsider policing and the narratives that have come to define the "war on crime," as well as the narratives that define persons of color as "nobody." The bottom line is this: people want to believe that the authority they are dealing with—let's say a police officer—believes that they matter—that they are Somebody.[220]

Creating Opportunities for Dialogue

While it has proven difficult to move beyond current narratives and to build trust between the police and residents in disadvantaged neighborhoods, difficult does not mean impossible. When residents believe they have been treated fairly and respectfully, they tend to grant more legitimacy to the police and are more likely to engage with them in problem solving around issues that threaten neighborhood safety and stability. A video from North Charleston, South Carolina, the city in which a police officer took the life of Walter Scott, an unarmed man of color, in 2015, demonstrates the efforts of the police department to change the narrative, by rebuilding support and collaborating with the community to address gun violence.[221]

The video identifies a distinct narrative: The North Charleston Police Department is committed to preventing and reducing violence, the police care, and the police are working with the community—not against them—in a united effort to reduce violence. The video is just one example of how police departments can use narrative, social media, and more importantly actions, to create opportunities for dialogue and collaboration to protect neighborhoods from violent crime.

In using "soft power," or in behavioral terms "attractive power," police departments can engage community members "left of conflict." Soft power uses a different type of currency

---

[219] Marc Lamont Hill, *NOBODY: Casualties of America's War on the Vulnerable, From Ferguson to Flint and Beyond* (New York: Atria Books, 2016).
[220] Angela J. Davis, *Poling the Black Man: Arrest, Prosecution and Imprisonment* (New York: Panteon Books, 2017), 165.
[221] City of North Charleston, "NCPD Marches for Homicide Victims," YouTube, uploaded on August 4, 2020, https://www.youtube.com/watch?v=ztPQi4iDo0Y.

(not force) to engender collaboration—an attraction to shared values, fairness, equity and the duty of contributing to the achievement of those values.[222] Research suggests that community-engaged policing has the potential to enhance police legitimacy. When persons view the police as legitimate legal authorities, they are more likely to cooperate and obey the law.[223] Judgements about the legitimacy of the police are influenced by narratives and actions that demonstrate the police are "acting in procedurally just ways."[224]

The Youth & Police Initiative (YPI) was developed by the North American Family Institute (NAFI) to help reduce youth violence and improve youth-community-police relations. In 2004, then Public Safety Commissioner Frank Straub implemented YPI in White Plains, New York in response to a youth-involved homicide and a series of retaliatory attacks that followed.

In a New York Times article from 2007, reporter Fernanda Santos, described a YPI session she observed:

> Like two tribes, they faced each other. One group wore the uniform of their trade: dark- blue outfits adored with shields and badges, guns tucked in leather holsters. The other donned what could be defined as the uniform of a generation: oversize pants, loose T- shirts, chains dangling from their necks... Unlike their previous encounters, this meeting at the Winbrook Apartments, the largest public housing complex in this city of 57,000, was not rooted in confrontation. Instead, a dozen police officers and an equal number of young men who live in or near the housing project convened for an exercise in understanding... At first glance, the group of officers, who are mostly white, and the youths, all of them black, seemed to have little in common. But soon similarities bubbled to the surface...[225]

YPI engages youth and families in positive social change to reduce violence and gang involvement by creating sustainable positive relationships among teens and adults of authority—especially police, school personnel, and civic leaders—replacing animosity and distrust with mutual respect and understanding:

---

[222] Joseph Nye, *Soft Power: The Means to Success in World Politics* (New York: Public Affairs, 2004), 7

[223] T.R. Tyler, *Why People Obey the Law: Procedural Justice, Legitimacy and Compliance* (New Haven: Yale University Press, 1990).

[224] President's Task Force on 21st Century Policing, *Final Report of the President's Task Force on 21st Century Policing* (Washington, DC: Office of Community Oriented Policing Services, 2015), 1.

[225] Fernanda Santos, "In a Room, Police and Youths Talk, and Maybe See Their Similarities," *New York Times*, June 29, 2007.

Officer Jason Lacayo… said he grew up in the Bronx and had friends who were in gangs, which prompted Derrick Ephraim… to confide that he was once in a gang himself. 'It's good to interact when the cops don't have their guards up,' said Mr. Ephraim, whose nickname, D Eagle, derives from the semiautomatic pistol Desert Eagle.

Over pizza and soda, the officers, who patrol the downtown area, and the young men, half of whom have been arrested or have served time in jail, talked candidly for five hours about baseball rivalries, college plans and the difficulties they face on the job and at home.[226]

The Youth Police Initiative includes a detailed curriculum and team building exercises that teach students life skills such as conflict resolution, responsibility, appreciating cultural diversity, and goal setting:

A rookie officer… who took part in the youth encounters said… 'it was good to talk to the kids, you know. They opened up to us, they saw we're human and their attitude changed. In a good way.'[227]

In White Plains, YPI contributed to a decline in crime and other disturbances at the Winbrook housing complex. Overall, reported crime in the city decreased by nearly 39 percent during the period 2002-2007. Additionally, during the period 2004-2010, there was not another youth-involved homicide or significant act of violence in the city.

Another video describes YPI and its impact on reconstructing youth and police narratives in the Franklin Field Housing Development in Boston, Massachusetts, creating opportunities for constructive dialogue and engagement.[228] Effective narrative strategies make it possible for the police to tell the story of who they are, what they are doing, and why they are doing it. Through effective story telling the North Charleston Police Department and other police departments that have participated in the Youth and Police Initiative are able to get out ahead of those who hope to fuel distrust. Instead, they frame events in a constructive manner

[226] Santos, "In a Room, Police and Youths Talk."
[227] Santos, "In a Room, Police and Youths Talk."
[228] Jay Paris, "Youth and Police Initiative Short Movie," Vimeo, uploaded on February 22, 2016, https://vimeo.com/156323441.

so that they can influence future interactions and reconstruct the narratives that have defined the reality of community—youth-police conflict.[229]

The President's Task Force on 21st Century Policing

In 2015, President Obama convened the Task Force on 21st Century Policing in the aftermath of the officer-involved death of Michael Brown and the protests that followed, in Ferguson and across the nation. In its opening paragraph, the President's Task Force acknowledged that "trust between law enforcement agencies and the people they protect and serve is essential in a democracy. It is the key to the stability of our communities, the integrity of our criminal justice system, and the safe and effective delivery of policing services."[230]

> Community policing starts on the street corner, with respectful interactions between a police officer and a local resident, a discussion that need not be related to a criminal matter. In fact, it is important that not all interactions be based on emergency calls or crime investigations.[231]

To move forward amidst the current challenges, we must begin on the street corner, in neighborhoods long challenged by poverty, a lack of opportunity, violence and hopelessness. Individual police officers must treat all persons they encounter with dignity and respect—as Somebody. They must give individuals a "voice" during encounters. Officers must be neutral and transparent in their decision making and convey trustworthiness in their motives and actions.[232] Changing the long-standing war narrative that has defined policing will take time, commitment, and the realization that "peace keeping" is about "humans interacting with humans." Day-to-day citizen interactions are where police legitimacy is reinforced or degraded. Every time a police officer is rude, condescending, sarcastic, or inattentive, police legitimacy takes a hit. By contrast, police officers that conduct themselves in a manner that

---

229 Ajit Maan, "Narrative Warfare," *RealClear Defense*, February 27, 2018, https://www.realcleardefense.com/articles/2018/02/27/narrative_warfare_113118.html.

230 President's Task Force on 21st Century Policing, *Final Report of the President's Task Force on 21st Century Policing* (Washington, DC: Office of Community Oriented Policing Services, 2015), 1.

231 President's Task Force, *Final Report*, 41.

232 President's Task Force, *Final Report*, 10.

conveys dignity and respect, even in the ugliest encounters, support the narrative that the police are committed to the procedurally just and fair maintenance of public safety and order.

In his seminal work, *Police: Streetcorner Politicians*, William Ker Muir, Jr. writes:

> A policeman becomes a good policeman to the extent that he develops two virtues. Intellectually, he has to grasp the nature of human suffering. Morally, he has to resolve the contradiction of achieving just ends with coercive means. A patrolman who develops this tragic sense and moral equanimity tends to grow in the job, increasing in confidence, skill, sensitivity, and awareness.[233]

While it is important to recognize that individual police officers play a critical role in neighborhood safety, narrative building, and communication—the vast majority of social control is informal in nature. The urbanist Jane Jacobs described social control this way:

> The first thing to understand is that the public peace—the sidewalk and street peace—of cities is not kept primarily by the police, necessary as the police are. It is kept primarily by an intricate, almost unconscious, network of voluntary controls and standards among the people themselves and enforced by the people themselves.[234]

When community policing is implemented effectively police officers create safe and stable environments that allow informal social control networks to take root, to grow, and support public peace.

Effective neighborhood-centric policing practices generate social capital and collective efficacy by bringing together diverse, sometimes antagonistic, elements of a community together by asking them to take a role in addressing issues and challenges. Collaboration and cooperation between the police and neighborhood residents improve relationships, generates feelings of trust, builds police legitimacy and changes the narrative of "us versus them" to one of engagement and consensus building—a strategic narrative of inclusion:

---

[233] William Ker Muir Jr., *Police: Streetcorner Politicians* (Chicago: The University of Chicago Press, 1977), 3–4.

[234] Jane Jacobs, *The Death and Life of Great American Cities* (New York: Vintage Books, 1961), 31.

> It is critical to help community members see police as allies rather than as an occupying force and to work in concert with other community stakeholders to create more economically and socially stable neighborhoods.[235]

With rigorous attention to neighborhood issues related to the social, environmental, economic, public health, education, crime and other contexts, as well as the timing and accumulation of risk, optimal moments for, and methods of intervention, can be identified and sustained over time. The collaborative and cooperative work of the police, residents, businesses, and other partners to address patterns of neighborhood disorder and crime provide opportunities to stimulate neighborhood revitalization, economic activity and safety:

> Collaborative approaches that engage professionals from across systems have emerged as model practices for addressing community problems that are not resolvable by the police alone. The team approach calls upon law enforcement agencies, service providers, and community support networks to work together to provide the right resources for the situation and foster sustainable change.[236]

Collaboration is a process in which organizations work together to attain common goals by sharing knowledge, learning, and building consensus. A collaborative approach enables law enforcement to build strategic initiatives and shape the narrative at the community level, versus being shaped by it. Police officials must articulate a narrative that explains and demonstrates to what end law enforcement action is being taken, and frame the narrative within the context of community-engaged policing.

It is clear, that neither individual police officers, nor the departments in which they serve, can fully protect neighborhoods from crime, and in fact, one-dimensional intensive law enforcement efforts to control crime, as discussed earlier, have proven to be deleterious to community relations, particularly in socially and economically disadvantaged neighborhoods. Many of the social problems that give rise to disorder and crime lie far outside police expertise and capabilities. Unfortunately, the police have been given the impossible task of "controlling" social problems created by an ecosystem of failing institutions, and too often, they are provided only one tool to do so, "the hammer of law." For the vast majority of social

[235] President's Task Force, *Final Report*, 42.
[236] President's Task Force, *Final Report*, 43.

problems, the police are often the default institution for people to call regardless of the neighborhood in which they live.[237] As Geoffrey Canada noted:

> Police officers are given a job to do which is impossible. It doesn't take them long to find out they are not going to erase crime, so they do the best they can, not really knowing what the overall plan is because there is no overall plan.[238]

Despite the impact of the President's Task Force on 21st Century Policing, research, and social experiments—there is no overall plan regarding the role of the police in America's neighborhoods. They remain the go to agency to not only control crime, but to deliver a host of mental and public health services to neighborhood residents. Yet, according to Friedman, the "police are barely trained in any of this, so it is no surprise harm is the result."[239]

The Police Response to Civil Unrest

> Race relations is a complicated collection of issues that touch on virtually every aspect of American life. When race relations explode into rioting, police action will almost certainly be the spark... While race riots occur in the context of a convoluted mix of social, economic, and cultural factors, policing consistently remains a crucial piece of the equation. It would be overreaching to designate police action as the sole factor in race riots; nevertheless, the importance of the police in preventing and effectively responding when disorder occurs can hardly be overstated.[240]

In the aftermath of George Floyd's death, we have seen images of heavily armed police officers deploying chemical and other munitions, using armored vehicles, and military-style equipment in response to the protests that have swept the nation. As law enforcement officers endeavor to protect civil rights, ensure public safety, and resolve conflict, we must pause and consider the use of "power" by law enforcement—hard, soft, and informational—in response to protests.

---

[237] Barry Friedman, "Disaggregating the Police Function," New York University School of Law, Public Law and Legal Theory Research Paper Series, Working Paper No. 20-03, April, 2020.
[238] Geoffrey Canada, *Fist Stick Gun: A Personal History of Violence in America* (Boston, MA: Beacon Press, 1995), 128.
[239] Friedman, "Disaggregating the Police Function," 1.
[240] Howard Rahtz, *Race, Riots and the Police* (Boulder, CO: Lynne Rienner Publications, 2010), 1.

Protests are among the most difficult situations the police have to manage. In doing so, they must balance the 1st Amendment rights of the protestors with the safety of the public and officers.[241] Ideally, the persons leading or planning a demonstration would meet with the police to plan the event(s) together, specifying the times, locations, and activities that would happen, including arrests. However, today protests are more complex, spontaneous, and unpredictable than in the past, with numerous leaders, narratives, and agendas in the crowd often making it difficult for police officials to negotiate the "terms" of the demonstration.

Whenever possible, communication and de-escalation should be the first level of the law enforcement response to protests. Unfortunately, as we have seen—de-escalation and even longstanding relationships between local activists and the police do not guarantee that a protest will remain peaceful. In protests where agitators provoke violence, or where persons commit crimes amidst large crowds, confusion, and turmoil, the police must determine the appropriate level of force to use, recognizing that too much force can escalate the situation—but so can too little.

The law enforcement response to protests must be proportional to the actions of the protestors and consistent with the rule of law, their policies, procedures, and training. Additionally, law enforcement officials must recognize that they are in a "contest" with agitators to control the narrative and the dynamics of the crowd. Therefore, the police response to violence, criminal activity, and rhetoric must be disciplined, measured, and legitimate in the eyes of the protestors and the community.

A comprehensive crowd management plan includes officers equipped with personal protective equipment and the tools needed to disperse crowds that become violent and endanger public safety. However, it is important to recognize that once officers are deployed in personal protective equipment and force is used—a dangerous cycle can be created in which protestors escalate their actions toward the police, the police escalate further, and both sides become increasingly angry and aggressive. Therefore, law enforcement officers should only use force and deploy less-lethal devices in response to escalating violence and direct threats to public safety that could not be averted through other methods. When force is used, it must

---

[241] Shaila Dewan and Mike Baker, "Facing Protests Over Use of Force, Police Respond With More Force," *The New York Times*, May 31, 2020.

be closely monitored, used only until the threat is reduced, carefully documented, and discussed with the community. Transparency and accountability demonstrate procedural justice and support opportunities for constructive engagement.

Ultimately, the key to a successful protest management strategy involves credibility and narratives that describe police actions in a way that builds trust among the protestors, the communities in which they are taking place, and the nation. This is particularly difficult, but even more important, when the genesis of protest is an officer involved in shooting or use of force.

Narrative Strategy

Within the current protest environment, police leaders must move beyond standard press releases that simply provide facts and develop narrative strategies that deliver meaning to their actions. The police cannot allow "agitators" to control the meaning of events, factual or otherwise. To do so, the police must develop a narrative strategy that is both offensive and defensive. The narrative strategy must be coordinated to build resilience within "friendly audiences" and disrupt the arguments of those seeking to discredit the police and accelerate civil disorder.

The protest environment has become complex as there are a series of sub-narratives in play, all of which speak to the identities of different audiences, all portraying meaning, not necessarily the truth, and all delivered in a form that is intended to trigger behavior in the various audiences. Becoming proactive, controlling the narrative with honest and immediate reporting, must be the foundation of police strategy and action. Every action taken and the ramifications of police conduct must be explained by way of narratives so that they are not misunderstood or allowed to be manipulated by adversaries: "Influence done well is a complex and intricate choreography of actions, words and related activities."[242]

[242] Paul Cobaugh, "White Paper: A Five-Point Strategy to Oppose Russian Narrative Warfare," Homeland Security Today, May 13, 2018, https://www.hstoday.us/white-papers/83285.

Conclusion

The war narratives that defined criminal justice for more than forty years, the narratives of life in socially and economically disadvantaged neighborhoods, and the narratives acted out by police officers every day are replete with public and private storylines—stories of trauma, anger, and frustration. However, there are also stories of hope, engagement, and collaborative actions in cities like White Plains, Boston, and North Charleston. In these cities, and others across the country, people living in disadvantaged neighborhoods and people that put on a police uniform every day to keep them safe, have met on the street corner, engaged, collaborated, and brought peace amidst turmoil.

The protests that took place in cities across America challenged us to develop new narratives, narratives that recognize the harm that has been caused, that accept responsibility, and offer a new storyline of respect, procedural justice, and inclusion. We must change the way we police communities. We must define the mission and role of the police in disadvantaged neighborhoods as well as in neighborhoods of prosperity. It is clear that the police cannot be all things to all people—they need others to step-up and assist them in executing a public safety model that is community-centric and draws on professionals from public and mental health, education, economic development, and other government, private, and not-for-profit sectors. This way, they can engage and work collaboratively with the community to solve the problems that have challenged us for way too long:

> The transmission of trauma becomes the "mechanism" through which group "history repeats itself," or threatens to do so, and through which groups become "stuck" in time and are, thus, unable to change.[243]

The police, supported by elected officials, can no longer wait to react to the voices of protest. Rather, the police must develop and communicate narratives that clearly articulate their vision of community safety, their support for 1st Amendment protests, their commitment to the rule of law, and the actions they will take when persons violate the law and/or commit acts of violence directed at persons or property. Police action during protests, as well as in the

[243] M. Gerard Fromm, *Lost in Transmission: Studies of Trauma Across Generations* (New York: Routledge, 2012), 183.

course of providing police services to neighborhood residents, must be explained in effective narratives that engender support because they are tied to values, are fair and just.

In closing, it is incumbent that we break the transmission of trauma across generations by developing and taking actions that support narratives of hope, procedural justice, and inclusion. In the words of President Obama:

> America, this is our moment. This is our time. Our time to turn the page on the policies of the past. Our time to bring new energy and new ideas to the challenges we face. Our time to offer a new direction for the country we love.[244]

Note: The views expressed are those of the author and do not necessarily reflect those of the National Police Foundation.

[244] Caren Bohan, "Obama Declares Victory," *Reuters*, June 3, 2008.

Chapter 9

Rethinking Strategy and Statecraft for the Information Age: Whose Narrative Wins

David Ronfeldt and John Arquilla

Around the world, national-security and foreign-policy strategists are having difficulty adapting to the digital age. A rethinking is needed. For decades, countless writings have pointed this out—ours among them—and marginal improvements are being made. But it is time to urge a deeper rethinking in light of new threats and other challenges to so many societies, institutions, and cultures. The experts are not meeting these threats and challenges well enough. Nor are strategists looking ahead the best ways possible.

It is not simply a technological matter—advanced information, communications, and sensing technologies are increasingly available. Instead, the challenge is mainly cognitive. Adversaries everywhere—from nations to nonstate networks—are using dark new modes of political, social, cultural, and psychological warfare against their opponents: wars of ideas, battles of stories, weaponized narratives, memetic viruses, and epistemic attacks. New kinds of cognitive warfare are being deliberately designed to confound analytic and social strengths and exploit weaknesses in individuals, institutions, and societies as a whole.

Strategists of all stripes—theorists and practitioners—remain unsettled and often baffled about how best to analyze, organize, and act amid this stormy flux. Trends and indications around the world suggest that matters may grow worse before they become better—*if* they do become better—in the coming years.

The most advisable way ahead for information-age strategists, especially in the world's capitals, is to reposition statecraft and grand strategy by merging two streams of thought: the first involves the well-known distinction between hard power and soft power; the second engages a lesser-known distinction about the geosphere, biosphere, and noosphere (the last term means "realm of the mind," as we clarify below). At first glance, the two streams may seem unrelated; but they are starting to come together in ways that should be recognized—the sooner the better. Doing so reveals a new kind of information-age statecraft we call "noopolitik" as a successor to traditional "realpolitik."

Hard Power Versus Soft Power

Strategists have traditionally thought and planned primarily in terms of tangible, material, "hard" forms of power—military forces, economic capabilities, and natural resources. They refined "realpolitik" in the 19th and 20th centuries to express their hard-power dispositions as a mode of statecraft that emphasizes seeking relative advantages through displays, threats, and uses of force. A realization that immaterial, ideational, "soft" forms of power—ideas, values, norms, and battles for hearts and minds—may matter as profoundly as "hard" forms of power started to take hold in the early 1990s, when the end of the Cold War and the relatively peaceful dissolution of the Soviet Union helped demonstrate the potential effectiveness of ideational approaches to statecraft. Hard power played a central role in deterrence and containment strategies from the 1940s to the 1980s; but it was the West's soft power (for example, the advocacy of democracy and free flows of information) that brought the decades of high-stakes confrontations to a successful, peaceful conclusion. Moreover, by then, the Internet and other digital information technologies were on the rise, and strategists, most of all in the United States, were beginning to view information itself as a new form of power, one that favored the "soft side" of the spectrum.

However, the American idea of soft power contained flaws. The original definition tended to treat soft power as good and hard power as bad, or at least as mean-spirited—i.e., soft power was said to be fundamentally about persuasive attraction, hard power about coercion.[245] But in actuality, soft power is not just about beckoning in attractive, upbeat, moralistic ways that make the United States and its allies, friends, and other like-minded societies look good. It can also be wielded in tough, dark, heavy ways too, as in psychological efforts to warn, embarrass, denounce, disinform, deceive, shun, or repel a targeted actor. Moreover, soft power does not inherently favor the good guys; malevolent leaders—say a

---

245 Joseph S. Nye, *Bound to Lead: The Changing Nature of American Power* (New York: Perseus Books, Basic Books, 1990); Joseph S. Nye, *Soft Power: The Means to Success in World Politics* (Cambridge, MA: PublicAffairs, 2004).

Hitler, a Bin Laden, or various of today's authoritarians—often prove eager and adept at using propagandistic soft-power measures in their efforts to dominate at home and abroad.

Thus, while strategists and other leaders in the more democratic societies were misconceiving the concept of soft power, even inflating it into "smart power" by combining hard and soft power,[246] they neglected to come up with a doctrinal derivative that could rival hard power's realpolitik; indeed, many simply persisted with realpolitik, trying to modify it to suit the information age. Spread over several decades, this conceptual inertia, even complacency, has left the United States, and quite often its allies and friends, at a strategic disadvantage. The American conceptual arsenal, not to mention those of its allies, is still sorely lacking for understanding about how to apply soft power. Strategists who believe primarily in hard power have developed quite a set of concepts around it, particularly over the past two centuries—e.g., realism, geopolitics, balance of power, and realpolitik itself. A comparable conceptual arsenal has yet to be developed around soft power.

Meanwhile, various adversaries and competitors of the West and other liberal societies—from nation-state actors like Russia, China, North Korea and Iran, to nonstate networks like Al Qaeda, the Islamic State (IS), and Wikileaks—quickly learned to develop dark approaches to soft power, especially online, in order to undermine American and other democracies and challenge their positions in the world. Thus, Moscow fielded new narratives to extol Eurasianism and deride democracy, while releasing a torrent of deception, disinformation, reflexive conditioning and de-truthing operations. And Beijing began concentrating on developing and deploying what it called "discourse power" as its way of influencing how people think about China and its growing reach around the world.

In short, democracy's adversaries began deploying aggressive soft-power strategies and tactics—lately called "sharp power"—far more adroitly than ever expected, catching Washington and other liberal capitals quite unawares and unprepared during the early years of the 21st century.[247] Nonetheless, rather than rethink matters, leaders in Washington and

---

[246] Nye, *Soft Power*.

[247] For "sharp power," see Christopher Walker and Jessica Ludwig, "The Meaning of Sharp Power: How Authoritarian States Project Influence," *Foreign Affairs*, November 16, 2017, https://www.foreignaffairs.com/articles/china/2017-11-16/meaning-sharp-power; Christopher Walker and Jessica Ludwig, "From 'Soft Power' to 'Sharp Power': Rising Authoritarian Influence in the Democratic World," in *Sharp Power: Rising Authoritarian*

elsewhere have continued to neglect America's soft-power capabilities; instead, they have reverted to re-emphasizing hard power and realpolitik.[248]

This state of affairs should be viewed with alarm—it should prompt an awareness of the urgent need to rethink statecraft for the information age. In our view, this means shifting away from realpolitik toward noopolitik, a concept inspired by a second stream of thought.

Emergence of the Noosphere

Over the past hundred years, various scientists in Europe, America, and Russia have worked on developing a stream of thinking about the geosphere, biosphere, and noosphere. Whether appearing singly or jointly, these three dimensions work as a set for understanding Earth's eons of evolution as a planet. Accordingly, first to evolve was a geosphere, consisting of the earth's geological mantle. Next to evolve was a similarly widespread biological layer, or biosphere, consisting of plant and animal life, eventually including people. Third to grow and develop will be an all-encompassing realm of the mind, a "thinking layer" termed the noosphere. These concepts were all in use by the 1920s, and continue to be today.[249]

The last term emerged when French theologian-paleontologist Pierre Teilhard de Chardin, his friend French mathematician Edouard Le Roy, and visiting Russian geochemist Vladimir Vernadsky met in Paris in 1922 to speculate about whether, because of humanity's growth, our planet would ultimately evolve a third layer: an all-enveloping noosphere, a term they coined from the Greek word "noos" meaning "the mind."[250] Teilhard defined it as a "realm of the mind," a "thinking circuit"—in the later words of his colleague, Julian Huxley, a "web of living thought" and "a common pool of thought" that would lead to an "inter-thinking humanity." For Teilhard, it was a spiritual as well as scientific concept; for Vernadsky, it was strictly a scientific concept—though both regarded it as having democratic political implications as well.

Influence, Washington, D.C., National Endowment for Democracy, International Forum for Democratic Studies, December, 2017, https://www.ned.org/sharp-power-rising-authoritarian-influence-forum-report.

[248] Andrew J. Bacevich, *Washington Rules: America's Path to Permanent War* (New York: Henry Holt and Company, 2010).

[249] For sources and citations regarding all quotes about the rise and spread of the noosphere concept, see David Ronfeldt and John Arquilla, *Whose Story Wins: Rise of the Noosphere, Noopolitik, and Information-Age Statecraft* (Santa Monica, CA: Rand, 2020), https://www.rand.org/pubs/perspectives/PEA237-1.html.

[250] For readings and background history about the rise and early spread of the noosphere concept, see Paul R. Samson and David Pitt, editors, *The Biosphere and Noosphere Reader: Global Environment, Society and Change* (New York: Routledge, 1999).

At first, the concept of the noosphere spread slowly and selectively among environmental scientists and social activists in the West. Some early believers are credited with helping to inspire the creation of the United Nations (UN), the United Nations Educational, Scientific and Cultural Organization (UNESCO), and other "noospheric institutions" after World War II. In addition, the postwar period led to UN-backed covenants that reflected noospheric hopes, such as the Universal Declaration of Human Rights and the Convention on the Prevention and Punishment of the Crime of Genocide, both in 1948. Not long after, the noosphere concept attracted wide attention in Europe and America in the 1950s and 1960s following the posthumous publication of Teilhard's books on *The Phenomenon of Man* and *The Future of Man*, as both became bestsellers. Even so, the concept still spread mostly among a narrow range of intellectuals—until the 1990s.

Since then, the rise of the Internet has excited a sense among myriad theorists and prophets of the information age that cyberspace is providing a technical foundation for the emergence of the noosphere. While the concept has still not gone mainstream, it is proliferating far and wide, now at the level of online platforms and not just individuals—*Wired* magazine, the *Edge* website, Evolution Institute, and various magazines and websites associated with pro-commons social theory and social activism on the Left often feature articles supporting the concept's potential. Indeed, from a political standpoint, people and platforms on the Left have shown the greatest interest in the noosphere and its future prospects. Interest on the Right is relatively rare. Theorists and activists on the Right are deeply interested in information-related concepts, systems, technologies, and their effects; but they prefer traditional constructs such as culture, ideology, and the media, maybe even atmosphere or zeitgeist, over noosphere or other futuristic notions.

Lately, various technologists and other scientists have preferred concepts that are not focused exactly on the noosphere: e.g., collective consciousness or the global brain. But they all still descend partly from the idea of the noosphere. Moreover, future successes with alternate concepts are bound to help further the noosphere too. It is here to stay; it will continue growing in significance and popular usage.

Onward Into the Future with Noopolitik

In sum, the noosphere concept provides logical grounding for thinking broadly about policy and strategy in the information age. Furthermore, our derivative concept—noopolitik—matches up with soft power, the way realpolitik matches up with hard power. No alternative concept does this as well—by comparison, cyberspace and the infosphere are smaller, more technological domains. The noosphere is the best all-encompassing concept for thinking about information-based realms and their dynamics.

We first proposed noopolitik as an alternative to realpolitik back in 1999.[251] But little happened then to further its development. Ever since, other strategists have proposed kindred concepts—notably, cyberpolitik, netpolitik, infopolitik, information engagement, information statecraft, information geopolitics—yet they too have failed to gain traction. Individually, these kindred concepts vary somewhat definitionally; but what is more important is that, collectively, they all represent innovative but so-far-unsuccessful efforts to improve the conceptual arsenals of strategists for dealing with information-age threats, challenges, and opportunities—in particular by urging strategists to emphasize networks more than hierarchies and nonstate actors as much as, sometimes more than state actors.

All of which leads to two points. First, noopolitik remains a suitable proposal for reorienting statecraft in the information age. Next, even if this particular concept does not take hold, strategists had better come up with something very similar, fast, before the world's dark adversaries do irreversible harm to the United States and other open societies by continuing to apply their own vexing mutations of noopolitik. At stake is the essence of effective strategy and statecraft in the information age: whose story wins.

Taken seriously, the noosphere concept has particular implications for developing noopolitik as an approach to statecraft. The noosphere began as a scientific and spiritual concept, but it has also acquired a forward-looking political cast. Its expansion implies the ascendance of ideational and other soft-power matters. It favors upholding ethical and

[251] John Arquilla and David Ronfeldt, *The Emergence of Noopolitik: Toward An American Information Strategy* (Santa Monica, CA: RAND, 1999), http://www.rand.org/pubs/monograph_reports/MR1033/index.html. See also David Ronfeldt and John Arquilla, "The Promise of Noöpolitik," *First Monday*, August 2007, http://firstmonday.org/ojs/index.php/fm/article/view/1971/1846; David Ronfeldt and John Arquilla, *Whose Story Wins: Rise of the Noosphere, Noopolitik, and Information-Age Statecraft*.

ecumenical values that seek harmony and goodwill, freedom and justice, pluralism and democracy, and a collective spirit harmonized with individuality. South Africa's Nelson Mandela and Desmond Tutu have served as exemplars to the world of this kind of value-driven statecraft.

Noopolitik is also a generally anti-war (though not pacifist) and pro-environment concept. Strategically, it implies thinking and acting in global/planetary ways while minding long-range ends, and the creation of new modes of agency to shape matters at all levels. It implies humanity coming together through all sorts of cognitive, cultural, and other close encounters. It is about the co-evolution of the planet and humanity—thus it implies understanding the nature of social and cultural evolution far better than theorists have so far. And it means engaging nonstate as well as state actors in a quest to create a new (post-Westphalian) model of world order less tethered to the nation-state as the sole organizing principle and focus of loyalty. Furthermore, it favors the widespread positioning of sensory technologies and the creation of sensory organizations for planetary and humanitarian monitoring and response purposes.

Yet, positive and peaceful as all this may seem, growth of the noosphere also implies having to deal with persistent ideational clashes and conflicts. Indeed, Teilhard, Le Roy, and Vernadsky said to expect ruthless struggles, shocks and tremors, even an apocalypse, as different parts of the noosphere begin to mingle and fuse around the world. These are not implications the founders simply tacked on; rather, they stem from discerning principles and dynamics that attended the prior development of the geosphere and biosphere as global envelopes.

Proponents and practitioners of noopolitik should heed these distinctive implications, and not view noopolitik as a self-aggrandizing public relations or propaganda game. When the switch to noopolitik deepens in the decades ahead, strategists will gradually figure out how different it is from realpolitik. For noopolitik requires a fresh way of looking at the world—a new kind of mindset, situational awareness, knowledge base, and assessment methodology, along with a generally more philosophical and theoretical outlook. How to look at hard power, thus realpolitik, is quite standardized by now. But how best to understand and use soft power is far from settled. Noopolitik depends on *knowing*—and finding new ways of knowing—

about ideational, cognitive, and cultural matters that have not figured strongly in traditional statecraft. As the information age deepens in the decades ahead, it will eventually be seen that noopolitik is not only an information-age alternative to realpolitik, but also a prospective evolutionary successor to it (see Table 1, which compares aspects of realpolitik and noopolitik).

Table 1. Contrast Between Realpolitik and Noopolitik

Realpolitik	**Noopolitik**
States as key units of analysis	States, nonstate actors, networks as key units
Primacy of national self-interests, sovereignty	Primacy of shared interests, mutuality
Primacy of hard power	Primacy of soft power
System as anarchic, conflictual	Harmony of interests, cooperation
Power politics as zero-sum game	Win-win as preferred game
Politics as unending quest for advantage	Politics as pursuing a *telos* (end purpose)
Alliances conditional (oriented to threat)	Alliance networks vital to security
Ethos is amoral, if not immoral	Ethics are crucially important
Behavior driven by interests, threats	Behavior driven by common values, goals
Balance of power as the "steady state"	Balance of responsibilities
Power embedded in nation-states	Power also embedded in "global fabric"
Guarded, manipulative about information	Seeks information-sharing, inter-thinking

In essence, noopolitik is ultimately about whose story wins—the power of narrative—not whose military seems stronger. This means that the conduct of noopolitik will depend on carefully crafting strategic narratives to suit varied contexts. The fact that narratives are crucial for maneuvering in today's world is widely accepted—as narrative strategist Ajit Maan has noted, "Kinetics may win battles; narratives win wars."[252] But designing strategic narratives remains more an art than a science, and there is still plenty of room for new ideas about how to build expertise and wield influence.

For example, U.S. efforts to promote democracy abroad—often through the use of force—have proceeded unsuccessfully, even defectively, for many years. The theologian

[252] Ajit Maan, "What We Do," Narrative Strategies website, 2017, https://www.narrative-strategies.com/what-we-do.

Reinhold Niebuhr, still a favorite philosopher of many conservative (as well as some liberal) strategists, cautioned back in the 1950s that "the greater danger [for U.S. strategy] is that we will rely too much on military strength"—a warning that has come all too true.[253] Given the sorry record of militarism, the matter of how best to promote democracy may well become a key opportunity for noopolitik; and the answer(s) and strategies that noopolitik may develop will likely prove quite different from what has been assumed and pursued under past grand strategies.

Here are some of the steps we have recommended to enable and energize a shift to noopolitik:

- Rethink "soft power," especially its dark sides: We should not have to list this; it should be cleared up by now—but it is not.
- Create international "special media forces" that could be dispatched into crisis and conflict zones to help settle disputes through the discovery and swift dissemination of accurate narratives, and for purposes of controlling rumors and improving transparency.
- Uphold "guarded openness" as a strategic principle: This means remaining open (particularly among allies) in accordance with democratic values, while also creating mechanisms for guardedness (e.g., mutual defense treaties, robust cybersecurity norms, disease detection and control early warning systems) to mitigate the risks inherent in being open.
- Take up the cause of protecting and managing the "global commons"—those air, sea, land, space, and other parts of our planet that belong to no single state or jurisdiction—as a pivotal issue area for the future of the noopolitik. Though valued by many civilian activists and military strategists, the global-commons concept has yet to gain public recognition, and it is presently under challenge from arch-traditionalists who prefer a return to nationalist/neo-mercantilist policies in the name of state sovereignty.
- Institute a governmental requirement for periodic reviews of the nation's "information posture": One's information posture toward allies and adversaries is now as crucial as one's military posture. The latter receives regular review; it is time to figure out how

[253] Reinhold Niebuhr, *The World Crisis and American Responsibility* (New York: Association Press, 1958), 35.

best to assess and enhance the national information posture as well. (If a national information posture assessment were conducted at this time by, for example, the United States, it would surely clarify that Washington is in strategically worse shape—on matters ranging from cybersecurity to America's standing in world opinion—than its regular military and economic posture assessments seem to indicate).

Such measures can open up transformational possibilities and opportunities for shifting from realpolitik to noopolitik as the basis of a new mode of statecraft attuned to the information age. They could help burnish the image of the United States and its allies and friends in the world once again, lessen the bitterness and violence of conflicts, revitalize diplomacy, especially public diplomacy, and set the world on course toward sustainable peace and prosperity. Whereas realpolitik treats international relations as intractably conflictual, the starting point for noopolitik is faith in upholding our common humanity, and a belief that, in statecraft, ideas can matter more than armaments.

Even now, many shifts, risks, and conflicts that are commonly categorized as geopolitical in nature are, on closer examination, primarily noopolitical. For example, during the past decade the Arab Spring—affecting countries from the Maghreb to the Levant—the rise of the Far Right in Europe, Hindu-Muslim clashes in South Asia, and protest movements in Venezuela, Sudan, Lebanon, Hong Kong, and Belarus all have geopolitical implications; but they may be better understood as having an essentially noopolitical nature. Around the world, many cognitive wars—ideological, political, religious, and cultural wars—are underway, aimed at shaping people's minds and asserting control over this or that part of the emerging noosphere. At the same time, people are also searching for new ways to get along together and cooperate in addressing such global challenges as climate change and refugee settlement. Here, too, policies and strategies guided by noopolitik rather than realpolitik will likely fare better for the common good.

New Frontiers for Teaching Statecraft and Grand Strategy

Colleges and universities have long offered courses, programs, and degrees in international relations and other topics that concern statecraft. However, those that focus specifically on grand strategy are quite recent. The first appeared only ten years ago, at Yale University, with the creation of its Brady-Johnson Program in Grand Strategy. Today not only Yale but also Duke University, the Massachusetts Institute of Technology (MIT), The Institute of World Politics (IWP), and a few other schools offer their own courses, programs, and degrees on grand strategy and statecraft.

For the most part, these courses revolve around classic readings in strategic thought and practice, from ancient Greece through modern times. They educate students about political, military, economic, social, and cultural forces that have affected international relations, often through assigned readings in military and diplomatic history. The focus is mostly on state-led strategies and policies across the centuries; but modern nonstate, citizen-activist, social-change movements may receive bits of attention too, as may the ways such movements benefit from the rise of new networked forms of organization enabled by the digital information revolution. Accordingly, class syllabi may range across writings by Thucydides, Niccolò Machiavelli, Carl von Clausewitz, Halford Mackinder, Hans Morgenthau, Henry Kissinger, et al. The list can be made very long when it extends to including writings by the latest crop of theorists and practitioners.

A very broad range of both hard- and soft-power factors may thus be covered. But, for the most part, the hard-soft distinction is not a major theme, except when including what is deemed the single essential reading on this topic: Joseph Nye's seminal book *Soft Power: The Means to Success in World Politics*.[254] Even so, these courses on grand strategy and statecraft generally cover the important roles that values, ideas, narratives, communications, culture, and other "soft" ideational factors may play in international relations, in peacetime as well as in war.[255] But much greater attention is usually devoted to educating students about strategic concepts that have grown around the "hard" material forms of power: e.g., geopolitics, realpolitik, realism, the use of economic coercion and military force, the balance of power,

[254] Joseph S. Nye, *Soft Power: The Means to Success in World Politics* (Cambridge, MA: PublicAffairs, 2004).

[255] Paul Kennedy, editor, *Grand Strategies in War and Peace* (New Haven: Yale University Press, 1991).

great-power competition, etc. Ever since Nye fielded the concept of "soft power" in the late 1990s, strategists have increasingly attended to the significance of soft-power factors, but not in systematic ways—no particular set of strategic concepts has yet arisen around it.

Suppose our forecast is correct about the noosphere and noopolitik. Then imagine how this may reshape curricula for graduate coursework on grand strategy. Current-day curricula seem quite staid, looking far more to the past than to what looms ahead. In recent decades, "realists" have run into theoretical and practical challenges that their conventional approaches to strategy have proved insufficient for characterizing or meeting, much less mastering. Classes and readings for educating about noopolitik will have to be very different from those used for realpolitik. Realpolitik requires knowing primarily about tangible military, economic, technological, and other geopolitical forces, and much less about intangible ideological, social, and cultural forces. In contrast, noopolitik requires knowing primarily about ideational, cultural, social, and other noopolitical forces—and finding new ways of knowing about them.

In the United States, strategic thinkers have long known, and urged, that grand strategy should attend to socio-cultural as well as political, military, technological, and other "hard" contextual factors. But, in practice, strategists have repeatedly neglected analyzing operational environments so comprehensively during the past few decades—they have neglected cultural and cognitive conditions to strategy's detriment, notably in Iraq and Afghanistan.[256] Calls are finally emerging for rethinking grand strategy so that it attends equally, and properly, to "the social dimension," including its domestic import for grand strategy.[257] A future turn toward noopolitik will require this.

A comprehensive guide for how to become a knowledgeable practitioner of noopolitik is unavailable at this time—the concept remains too new, the writings too few. Nonetheless, we can list some topics that will surely require elevated if not entirely new kinds of attention as the noosphere and noopolitik take hold. We discuss them briefly below, in order to suggest their prospective future importance for teaching and learning in forward-looking courses and

---

[256] Frank Hoffman, "Distilling The Essence Of Strategy," *War on the Rocks* blog, August 4, 2020, https://warontherocks.com/2020/08/distilling-the-essence-of-strategy; Thomas F. Lynch, editor, *Strategic Assessment 2020: Into a New Era of Great Power Competition* (Washington, DC: National Defense University Press, 2020).

[257] John Arquilla and Nancy Roberts, "How the Coronavirus Exposed the Flaws in America's Security Strategy," *The National Interest*, August 16, 2020, https://nationalinterest.org/feature/how-coronavirus-exposed-flaws-america%E2%80%99s-security-strategy-166830.

curricula about grand strategy. However, we expect that the topics we list here will eventually require far more pages of argument and elaboration before strategists steeped in traditional approaches become convinced that such a reorientation is needed.

• **Recognizing the significance of social evolution for grand strategy:** We have never seen a writing that explicitly pairs social evolution and grand strategy for analysis. Yet, grand strategies often rest on judgments about social evolution—who is gaining strength, progressing the best, becoming a model for others to follow, etc. Modern examples include containment theory in the 1950s, modernization theory in the 1960s, and democratic enlargement in the 1990s. During the 2000s, three ideas advanced during the previous decade that touched on social evolution theory—the "end of history," "the clash of civilizations," and "export of democracy" concepts—influenced strategists engaged in the "global war on terrorism," which became notable for its presumptuous naiveté about imposing a democratic political evolution on tribalized, strife-torn societies in Afghanistan and Iraq. Attempts to reroute the currents of history and culture in these sad lands have foundered, at terrible human and material cost.

What a grand strategist thinks (or dismisses) about social evolution can make a decisive difference. Indeed, a case can be made that grand strategy would benefit immensely if it were grounded in better theory about social evolution. This may seem a passing matter for realpolitik, but it may be a requisite concern for noopolitik—better ideas about social evolution will be needed in the coming age of the noosphere. Grand-strategic thinking that ignores social-evolutionary dynamics will not be worth much for long (especially for such purposes as fighting terrorism and promoting democracy). The fact that there is no agreed-upon theory of social evolution does not obviate this concern.

Exactly what a noopolitik-oriented curriculum should include is not clear today; but the aim would be to educate students to think more deliberately about social evolution and its implications for grand strategy, without opting necessarily for a particular framework or theory. To this end, readings by Peter Turchin and David Sloan Wilson may be advisable, along with selected writings by David Ronfeldt.[258] Readings on specific topics—e.g., the evolution of government institutions, market systems, political democracy, and civil-society networks—may also deserve inclusion.

• **Realizing the significance of social cognition for grand strategy:** According to realpolitik, strategy is the art of relating ends, ways, and means—usually as defined in hard-power terms.[259] Strategy from a noopolitik perspective will be more about identifying, assessing, and affecting peoples' cognitions, a soft-power concept. Assuming that peoples' key cognitions are about space, time, and agency, strategy may then be seen as an art of positioning for spatial, temporal, and agency-oriented advantages. For noopolitik, this may mean thinking and acting in global/planetary ways (spatially), while minding long-range future end-states (temporally), and creating new modes of action to shape matters at all scales of deliberate (i.e., agency-driven) activity.

Why focus on people's space, time, and agency (or action, or efficacy) cognitions? Because numerous psychological, sociological, anthropological, and other studies have shown that people's key cognitions are about space, time, and action (or agency). These cardinal cognitions—space, time, action—take form in people's minds during childhood, and play key roles in shaping their beliefs and behaviors from then on. They are essential building blocks behind the development of consciousness and culture. No mind, culture, or society can function without its particular set of space, time, and action cognitions. Moreover, changes in people's space-time-action cognitions—their worldviews and mindsets—can lead to changes not only in an individual's beliefs and behaviors, but also in how a mass public thinks and acts collectively throughout an entire culture and society.

Thus, the better strategists can find ways to analyze people's space-time-action perceptions, the better they can ascertain why people think and behave as they do, how

[258] Peter Turchin, *Ultrasociety: How 10,000 Years of War Made Humans the Greatest Cooperators on Earth* (Chaplin, CT: Beresta Press, 2016); David Sloan Wilson, *This View of Life: Completing the Darwinian Revolution* (New York: Pantheon Books, 2019); David Ronfeldt, *Tribes, Institutions, Markets, Networks: A Framework About Societal Evolution* (Santa Monica, CA: RAND, 1996), https://www.rand.org/pubs/papers/P7967.html; David Ronfeldt, "Explaining Social Evolution: Standard Cause-and-Effect vs. TIMN's System Dynamics," *Materials for Two* Theories blog, September 18, 2009, http://twotheories.blogspot.com/2009/09/explaining-social-evolution-standard.html.

[259] Gabriel Marcella and Stephen O. Fought, "Teaching Strategy in the 21st Century," *Joint Forces Quarterly*, no. 52 (1st quarter, 2009): 56–60, https://apps.dtic.mil/sti/pdfs/ADA515184.pdf.

societies and cultures evolve, and what makes one historical era or phase different from another. Through such learning, strategists will be better positioned to assess the effects that different strategic options may have.

Today, it would not be easy to design courses and curricula to educate students about the significance of multidimensional cognitive analysis for grand strategy. Most experts have specialized in just one of the three key cognitions, in isolation from the others (even though the others always creep into their analyses). For the time being, courses and curricula would have to rely mainly on single-focus studies—say, Philip Zimbardo's writings about time orientations, or Albert Bandura's about efficacy orientations.[260] But they should still head steadfastly in the direction of multidimensional cognitive analysis until new readings emerge (as argued and forecast in writings by David Ronfeldt).[261]

• **Finding ways to assess and improve national information postures:** The United States has, over the past 75 years, provided an illuminating example of a sustained governmental effort to craft information strategy and policy, though it has yet to call for regularly assessing its "information posture" the way it has its military posture. Nevertheless, the American government does have a history of treating the nation's de facto information posture seriously—just not under that name. A modern landmark arose in 1946 with George Kennan's seminal "containment" concept, which was meant to be applied more in the ideational than the military realm. Later, in 1953, President Dwight Eisenhower created the United States Information Agency (USIA), and always included its director in cabinet-level meetings. As another landmark event, President Ronald Reagan ("the Great Communicator") called on his administration in March 1984, with his National Security Decision Directive 130, to develop a formal information strategy and posture review process. He then used it to help guide his

---

[260] Philip Zimbardo and John Boyd, *The Time Paradox: The New Psychology of Time That Will Change Your* Life (New York: Free Press, 2008); Albert Bandura, "Toward a Psychology of Human Agency," *Perspectives on Psychological Science* 1, no. 2 (2006): 164–180, https://www.uky.edu/~eushe2/Bandura/Bandura2006PPS.pdf.

[261] David Ronfeldt, "People's Space-Time-Action Orientations: How Minds Perceive, Cultures Work, and Eras Differ," draft, November, 2018, https://papers.ssrn.com/sol3/papers.cfm?abstract_id=3283477.

summitry with Premier Mikhail Gorbachev and end the Cold War. Quite a set of accomplishments!

But after the Cold War ended, President George H. W. Bush did not see fit to extend Reagan's initiative, preferring instead to proclaim an American-led "new world order" based on preponderant military and economic strength. And in 1999 President Bill Clinton disestablished the USIA as an independent entity (it was folded into the State Department, where it remains today, much weakened). Thus, the U.S. government began turning its back on developing a formal information posture at the very time when the digital information revolution was getting underway. "Information" was already being reconceptualized as a new form of power, but mostly by state and nonstate competitors who were intensifying their usage of new information operations against the United States, its allies and friends—without American or other friendly policymakers and strategists adequately realizing much of any of this.

Today, new voices are calling on the U.S. government to revitalize the USIA and rekindle the process that Reagan so wisely developed in 1984. These are good ideas. But far more than a limited institutional renaissance in one country—the United States is still too enamored of trying to impress other societies with its hard-power capabilities—will be needed in order to assure that policymakers begin to require national information-posture assessments as a regular matter.

Posture assessments are normally about a nation's capabilities to apply all manner of power on behalf of its national interests—the case with U.S. national military, economic, and cybersecurity assessments. They are supposed to identify a nation's strengths and weaknesses, its priorities and possibilities, as well as vulnerabilities and risks, so that a nation's leaders become better informed to craft strategies for meeting the ideational, organizational, operational, and other challenges that lie ahead.

To our knowledge, no one has ever tried to do a formal national information posture assessment. It could prove daunting as well controversial to undertake. To begin, "information power" and "information posture" (not to mention "information space") are far from settled concepts. But if they could be broadly defined, spanning ideational as well as material aspects of "information" (as we think they should be), then a posture assessment might be well advised to cover the following:

— key aspects of a nation's image (the "face" it presents to the world, its "brand identity"), in particular the national values, goals, character, and the reputation it means to uphold and project, at home and abroad;
— the wealth (or lack) of information resources a nation has at its disposal and is developing (or failing to retain and develop) in schools, universities, research centers, libraries, and elsewhere in the "infosphere," including in the nation's civil, public, and private sectors;
— the information policies and practices a nation favors, for example "freedom of information" and "guarded openness" in the American case;
— the status of infrastructures pertaining to stocks and flows of information, including the ways access is distributed or concentrated, management is centralized or decentralized, ownership and intellectual property are proprietary or shareable, and whether the designs are suited to meeting national needs in case of emergency;
— the information-monitoring and -sharing networks that exist for coordination and cooperation across all levels of government, domestic and foreign, as well as with IGOs and NGOs around the world on all manner of issues, and with business and civil-society actors at home;
— the range of media that are used for information gathering and broadcasting, as well as for uses that may range from message projection to early warning.

Such an assessment should identify strengths and weaknesses in a nation's information posture, its points of resilience and vulnerability in case of an attack or other disaster. It should consider how well the posture serves to attract and work with friends and allies, as well as to deter adversaries. It should set priorities and specify options for future improvements.

Today, the idea of formally assessing and improving a nation's information posture is so new, and so lacking in background materials, that it would be difficult to design educational courses and curricula. Yet it is too significant a topic to set aside. So, for now, it may be best to approach the topic via exploratory workshops, rather than instructional classes. It may also be advisable for such workshops to try to design ways for all governments to eventually produce information-posture assessments, not just one's own government (or other entity).

• **Additional topics for education in noopolitik:** The preceding three topics are easy to suggest, for they derive from our recent work. Yet they are just a beginning; other topics could easily be added to this list. For instance, the significance of strategic narratives—in light of the centrality of "whose story wins" to noopolitik, future strategists should receive training in the construction and application of forward-looking strategic narratives. Knowing more about social evolution, social cognition, and information postures, as recommended above, can help; but formulating narrative strategies involves a much wider range of skills for addressing people's distinctive psychologies, values, cultures, and histories, as all the chapters in this special volume attest.[262]

Another topic might be the growing significance of having (and building far more) networks of sensory technologies and sensory organizations around the world to monitor, share, and act on information about global health, education, environment, and other critical matters that cross jurisdictional boundaries. At first, this may sound like a mostly technical matter. But no, for this topic will prove to be mostly about designing and building vast organizational networks that involve all sorts of state and nonstate actors, large and small, near and far. Thus, as the noosphere and noopolitik grow in tandem, organizational races to build networks may well prove more important than the technological races to build ever newer products and weapons, catalyzed by the digital information revolution.

Coda

New courses and curricula for such matters would make for a very different, far more future-oriented approach to educating students about statecraft and grand strategy attuned to the decades ahead. To our knowledge, such matters are not being addressed much, neither singularly nor collectively, if at all, in today's institutions of higher learning. Moreover, the

[262] In addition to this volume, also see Ajit Maan, *Narrative Warfare* (Washington, DC: Narrative Strategies Ink, 2018) and other publications associated with Narrative Strategies Ink.

ideas and observations we have offered here are preliminary—for example, further discussion should surely lead to more refined ways to do a national information posture assessment. Yet, if our forecasts about the rise of the noosphere and noopolitik are correct, then it is already past time we all begin exploring and adapting to these new frontiers.[263]

[263] For useful review comments along the way, the authors thank Linda Akers, Peter Layton, Ajit Maan, and Gabriel Marcella. This chapter is adapted from a think-piece with a similar title, licensed under Creative Commons CC BY 4.0, as posted at http://twotheories.blogspot.com/2020/10/rethinking-strategy-and-statecraft-for.html.

List of Contributors

Ajit Maan, Ph.D. is a narrative strategist focused on the non-kinetic aspects of counter-terrorism, defense, and stability. She is Founder and CEO of the award-winning think-and-do-tank Narrative Strategies. She is also Faculty at the Center for the Future of War, Member of the Brain Trust of the Weaponized Narrative Initiative, and Professor of Practice in Politics and Global Security at Arizona State University. In addition to being a regular contributor to *Homeland Security Today*, she is author of several books including *Counter-Terrorism: Narrative Strategies, Narrative Warfare*, and *Plato's Fear*.

Howard Gambrill Clark, Ph.D. has specialized in influence strategies and psychological warfare for over 22 years. He graduated from Yale University with a degree in international relations focusing on the Middle East. While a student, Dr. Clark was a writer for U.S. Information Agency's Middle East/South Asia Division; served on the staff of the Senate Defense Appropriations Subcommittee; and studied Arabic at the American University in Cairo via a Department of Defense grant.

After Yale, Dr. Clark served as policy analyst in the Executive Office of the President for the President's Chief Economic Adviser, focusing on counterterrorism. Following the White House, Dr. Clark served in the U.S. Marine Corps as an intelligence officer and multi-national/special-unit commander with multiple deployments to Iraq as well as Afghanistan and the Philippines.

After military service, Dr. Clark was presidentially appointed as Department of Homeland Security Chief Intelligence Officer's Special Assistant. Then, as Senior Intelligence Analyst for Homeland Security Counter-Radicalization, Dr. Clark helped lead the Intelligence Community in intelligence support to countering violent (headquarters) before acting as consultant (contracted Senior Intelligence Analyst) to Special Operations Command's Counter-Radicalization Branch.

While earning his Ph.D. from King's College London War Studies, he served as senior counter-violent-extremism adviser and trainer for USAID, USSOCOM, USDA, DOS, Special

Forces, USMC, NATO, and partner governments in southwest Asia, and Associate Fellow at the International Centre for the Study of Radicalisation.

He is now the president of Narrative Strategies, where he teaches and researches the fields of strategic influence, psychological warfare, counterterrorism, and countering violent extremism. He is also an associate professor of influence strategy and psychological warfare in Washington, DC.

Lieutenant Colonel (Retired) Brian L. Steed, Ph.D. is a retired US Army lieutenant colonel with more than thirty years of civilian and uniformed experience. He is a practitioner, student, and writer of military theory, Middle East culture, and history.

Brian is an associate professor of military history at the U.S. Army Command and General Staff College where he was the 2018 Military Educator of the Year. He is also a senior fellow at Narrative Strategies. As an Army officer, he was a Middle East foreign area officer, which included eight and a half consecutive years living and working in the Middle East, to include assignments in Jordan, Israel, Iraq, and the United Arab Emirates. Brian holds a Ph.D. from the University of Missouri-Kansas City in political science and history.

Brian has written and edited numerous books, articles, and papers on military theory, military history, and cultural awareness. His most recent books include *ISIS: The Essential Reference Guide*, *Iraq War: The Essential Reference Guide* (editor), *ISIS: An Introduction and Guide to the Islamic State*, *Voices of the Iraq War: Contemporary Accounts of Daily Life (Voices of an Era)* (editor), and *Bees and Spiders: Applied Cultural Awareness and the Art of Cross-Cultural Influence*.

Brigadier General (Retired) Tom Drohan, Ph.D., JMark Services' International Center for Security and Leadership Director, is a retired U.S. Air Force brigadier general and professor emeritus of military and strategic studies, US Air Force Academy. His 38-year career as a pilot and professor included operational campaigns and commands, undergraduate and graduate-level teaching, and educational leadership. His academic experience includes a B.S. focused on national security studies (USAF Academy), M.A. in political science (University of Hawaii), Ph.D. in politics (Princeton University), Council on Foreign Relations fellowship in Japan, mentor at the National Military Academy of Afghanistan, visiting scholar at the Reischauer Center for East Asian Studies (Johns Hopkins School of Advanced International Studies), dean of the U.A.E. National Defense College, and 27 years of teaching. He is the author of *American-Japanese Security Agreements* (McFarland & Co., 2007) and *A New Strategy for Complex Warfare* (Cambria Press, 2016). He actively contributes to security and defense-related journals.

Mr. Paul Cobaugh retired from the US Army as a Warrant Officer after a distinguished career in the U.S. Special Operations CT community, primarily focused on mitigating adversarial influence and advancing U.S. objectives by way of influence. Throughout his career he has focused on the centrality of influence in modern conflict, whether it be from extremist organizations or state actors employing influence against the U.S. and our Allies. Post military career he accepted the position of Vice President at Narrative Strategies, a U.S. based Think-Do Tank which specializes in the non-kinetic aspects of conflict. He has also co-authored *Soft Power on Hard Problems* (Hamilton Publishing, 2017), *Introduction to Narrative Warfare: A Primer and Study Guide* (Narrative Strategies Ink, 2018), and *Modern-Day Minutemen and Women or… how to save the 2020 Election* (Narrative Strategies Ink, 2020).

Aleksandra Nesic, Ph.D., serves as a visiting Senior Social Scientist and Faculty at the U.S. Army's J.F.K. Special Warfare Center and School, where she develops and teaches new courses in the advanced interdisciplinary science of the human domain. She is also a Visiting Faculty in the Countering Violent Extremism and Combatting Transregional Terrorism Fellowship Programs at the Joint Special Operations University (USSOCOM), Tampa, Florida, and a Senior Lecturer at the Foreign Service Institute at the U.S. Department of State. She is a founding partner and a Senior Researcher at Valka-Mir Human Security, LLC, a research firm that specializes in population intelligence. Dr. Nesic holds a Ph.D. in International Conflict Analysis and Resolution, a Master's degree in Intercultural Communication and Education, a Postgraduate Certificate in Conflict Transformation and

Peacebuilding, and a Bachelor of Science in Psychology. Dr. Nesic's ongoing research examines the formation and spread of violent extremist ideologies and recruitment strategies employed by various non-state actors, Russian and Chinese global influence operations, as well as the development of psychological resilience mechanisms for individuals and communities vulnerable to extremist recruitment.

Colonel (Retired) Christopher Holshek is an international peace and security consultant and a senior civil-military advisor at Narrative Strategies, the Alliance for Peacebuilding, and U.S. Global Leadership Coalition "Veteran for Smart Power." As such, he promotes transversal civil-military narratives on cross-cutting national and international peace and security issues, through learning co-development and his writings. Much of his work draws from his National Service Ride project to empower citizenship and service to help move a divided nation forward, based on his book *Travels with Harley—Journeys in Search of Personal and National Identity* (Inkshares, 2016). He is also a civil-military advisor for a NATO Partnership & Cooperative Security Committee research and development project on "Resilient Civilians in Hybrid and Population-Centric Warfare." As vice-president for the Civil Affairs Association, he develops and organizes intellectual capitalization platforms for U.S. civil affairs force development and edits the *Civil Affairs Issue Papers*. A rare American with UN field mission service in civilian and military capacities in the Balkans and Africa, he is the principal author of the Peace Operations Training Institute's course on civil-military coordination in peace operations. A retired U.S. Army Civil Affairs officer with over three decades of civil-military conflict management experience at multiple levels and settings across the full range of operations, his assignments included: command of the first Civil Affairs battalion deployed to Iraq in support of Army, Marine and British forces; Chief of Civil-Military Coordination for the UN Mission in Liberia; and European Command Military Representative at the U.S. Agency for International Development. For his services then and since, he was inducted as a Distinguished Member of the Civil Affairs Regiment (Corps) in 2017. He was also a senior associate with the Project on National Security Reform. In addition to his contributions to U.S. Army, Joint, NATO, and UN civil-military and peace & stability operations policy and doctrine, he has published in numerous formats on national strategy, civil-military, humanitarian, and peace & stability operations issues, including *Foreign Policy*, *The Huffington Post*, and *Sicherheit & Frieden*.

Frank G. Straub, Ph.D., is the Director of the National Police Foundation's Center for Mass Violence Response Studies (CMVRS). Dr. Straub works with police departments and communities throughout the country on a variety of issues and challenges, conducting after action assessments of mass violence attacks and 1st Amendment protests, providing technical assistance, and training. He leads the national Averted School Violence project and works closely with police and community groups to counter violent extremism.

Dr. Straub is a 30-year veteran of local, state and federal law enforcement, having served as the Police Chief in Spokane, Washington; the Public Safety Director in Indianapolis; the Public Safety Commissioner in White Plains, New York; and the New York City Police Department's Deputy Commissioner of Training and Assistant Commissioner for Counterterrorism. During his career, he received national recognition for the community-involved programs he implemented to reduce crime, youth violence, and improve the police response to persons challenged by mental illness and developmental disabilities.

Dr. Straub holds a B.A. in Psychology, a M.A. in Forensic Psychology, and a Ph.D. in Criminal Justice. He is a Non-Resident Fellow at Combatting Terrorism Center at the U.S. Military Academy, West Point; a member of Yale University's Workgroup on Social Isolation and Extremism; and, a Graduate Faculty Scholar in the University of Central Florida, Department of Psychology.

David Ronfeldt, Ph.D., now retired, worked for more than 35 years at the RAND Corporation as a political scientist. His work resulted in new ideas about information-age modes of conflict (cyberwar, netwar, swarming), future security strategy (guarded openness, noopolitik), and social theory (nascent frameworks for analyzing social evolution and social cognition). He has a Ph.D. in political science.

John Arquilla, Ph.D., is distinguished professor of defense analysis at the Naval Post-Graduate School. Beyond his work with David Ronfeldt, his books include *The Reagan Imprint* (2006), *Insurgents, Raiders, and Bandits* (2011), and *Why the Axis Lost* (2020). He has a Ph.D. in political science. While at RAND, Ronfeldt and Arquilla coauthored many reports, including *In Athena's Camp: Preparing for Conflict in the Information Age* (1997), *The Zapatista "Social Netwar" in Mexico* (1998), *The Emergence of Noopolitik: Toward an American Information Strategy* (1999), *Swarming and the Future of Conflict* (2000), and *Networks and Netwars: The Future of Terror, Crime, and Militancy* (2001).